Overcoming Cultural Mismatch

Overcoming Cultural Mismatch

Reaching and Teaching Diverse Children

Abigail L. Fuller

ROWMAN & LITTLEFIELD
Lanham • Boulder • New York • London

Published by Rowman & Littlefield
An imprint of The Rowman & Littlefield Publishing Group, Inc.
4501 Forbes Boulevard, Suite 200, Lanham, Maryland 20706
www.rowman.com

6 Tinworth Street, London SE11 5AL, United Kingdom

British Library Cataloguing in Publication Information Available

Library of Congress Cataloging-in-Publication Data

Names: Fuller, Abigail L., 1982– author.
Title: Overcoming cultural mismatch : reaching and teaching diverse
   children / Abigail L. Fuller.
Description: Lanham : Rowman & Littlefield, [2021] | Includes
   bibliographical references. | Summary: "This book provides actionable
   steps for educators to take to commit to the immediate inclusion of
   diversity, working toward culturally responsive teaching"—Provided by
   publisher.
Identifiers: LCCN 2021011188 (print) | LCCN 2021011189 (ebook) | ISBN
   9781475862034 (cloth) | ISBN 9781475862041 (paperback) | ISBN
   9781475862058 (epub)
Subjects: LCSH: Culturally relevant pedagogy. | Inclusive education.
Classification: LCC LC1099 .F85 2021 (print) | LCC LC1099 (ebook) | DDC
   370.117—dc23
LC record available at https://lccn.loc.gov/2021011188
LC ebook record available at https://lccn.loc.gov/2021011189

~

Contents

~

Foreword

As a retired teacher, having taught for forty years, I found this book to be filled with invaluable research that will be beneficial for everyone involved, especially our diverse student population. I have always believed that for *every* student the sky is the limit. It gives me great joy knowing that Dr. Fuller was led to share such precious findings with teachers, who can make or break a student's desire to succeed academically as well as socially. I met Dr. Fuller during her years as an assistant principal of an elementary school where I served as a kindergarten teacher of diverse students. Throughout the school there were cultural mismatches.

Overcoming Cultural Mismatch: Reaching and Teaching Diverse Children is a must read in that it provides teachers with resources to obtain the tools needed to effectively reach and teach students who are culturally diverse. Being knowledgeable about these cultural differences and implementing them in the culturally diverse classroom will ensure a positive change in academic and social development. These changes can be achieved with ease once the findings are applied in the classroom. The teacher will then be able to encourage the students to "reach for the stars." As teachers, our goal should be for every student to succeed.

Overcoming Cultural Mismatch reminds us that the content of what is taught is important; however, it is the *how* of what is taught that determines the success of the recipient, that is, the comprehension. This book is filled with scientific research that promotes the importance of cultural awareness as it relates to instructing students of diverse cultures.

Many minorities have long been perceived as underachievers. The findings in this book will give teachers the opportunity to gain crucial knowledge that can help change this misconception. As is stated here, knowing a student's culture can enable one to enhance the learning environment so that the student feels confident about his or her ability to achieve.

Thanks to Dr. Fuller for having the insight to complete such a study. She saw the importance of addressing the need for teachers to educate themselves about different cultures for the purpose of providing the ultimate learning environment for everyone. Implementation of these findings will support teachers' endeavors to assure students that the sky is indeed the limit. *Overcoming Cultural Mismatch* provides the necessary tools to make achievement possible for every student. Teachers, encourage each and every one of your students to reach for the sky. It is attainable.

Marie C. Perry

Preface

At the end of a presentation I was giving in Norfolk, Virginia, a woman in her first few years of teaching said to me, "I signed up for your workshop because the topic sounded interesting, but when I got here, I thought, 'Ugh, another white lady talking about culturally responsive teaching and telling us how to teach minority students,' but then you shared about your husband and your own children, and about teachers creating a cultural autobiography, and I realized how relevant your work is." (The elephant in the room is now removed.)

A white, monolingual female originally from a small town in the northeastern United States, I was the individual who research states may not be able to reach and teach every child, specifically those with cultural backgrounds different from my own. I decided during my undergraduate teacher preparation coursework to step out of my comfort zone and into a world of diversity through personal, philanthropic, and teaching experiences. Increased knowledge, personal growth, and reflection have led me to a career teaching and advocating for underrepresented populations.

With intentions of reaching and teaching every child I would encounter as an elementary school teacher, setting a personal goal to overcome cultural mismatch in my own classroom was just the beginning. My career has evolved to conducting research, teaching, and supervising preservice teachers in a university teacher preparation program to impart to aspiring teachers the changing demographics in U.S. schools and the likelihood of teaching culturally diverse students. I am a certified teacher and certified educational leader.

The desire to write this book stems from my background as an educational professional, having worked as a school administrator, special education specialist, and teacher. This includes years of experience with students of racial, ethnic, cultural, and socioeconomic diversity and their parents. My goal is to best prepare preservice teachers to effectively educate students of all backgrounds. Teachers who are more knowledgeable about diversity can work to increase the achievement of all students in America's schools, with a particular focus on minority and impoverished students.

Providing teachers and administrators with practical solutions for inclusive schools and preparing preservice teachers to effectively teach diverse students are two of my pursuits and a goal of this book. As a white female in the field of education, I relate firsthand to the literature on cultural mismatch. Furthermore, my cultural experiences frame my career and research interests. These influences include urban school teaching internships, teaching at Title I–funded schools, completing graduate coursework on diversity and social justice, personally living a bicultural life with my family, and my belief that all children are created in the perfect image of God.

Accustomed to more than one culture, I am married to an African American man who is also a teacher. My perspectives about race and culture are very conscious, affect my interactions and relationships with others, and serve as my lens for viewing the world and my decision making. My family and I have personally experienced racism, stereotyping, and discrimination related to our interracial family and my husband and children's brown skin. Because of this, I know firsthand that bias exists and can cause actions that are sometimes intentionally hateful, unfortunately, yet most times unintentional.

As a result, I am interested in further understanding the perceptions of minority students who are marginalized populations in U.S. public schools to address the inequities that exist and provide relevant learning opportunities for students. I chose to write this book, in part, as a call to action and a guide for preservice and practicing teachers and school leaders to understand and overcome cultural mismatch, ultimately helping every child reach his or her potential in school.

I invite teachers and school leaders to join me on the journey of culturally responsive teaching. Regardless of one's background and experiences, preservice and practicing teachers can reflect on their own culture and bias related to diversity and teaching diverse students through writing a cultural autobiography.

My respective case study research on 1) exploring students' perceptions of their teacher's cultural responsiveness, and 2) exploring preservice teachers' perceptions of creating a cultural autobiography and readiness to teach diverse students illustrates the need for preservice teachers, practicing teachers, and school leaders to know and understand cultural mismatch and its negative effects. The most significant pieces of these cases is the perceptions, or voices, of students in the first case and the voices of preservice teachers in the second.

These studies add to the discourse on culturally responsive teaching and create a platform for the voice of the student to be heard in pre-K through 12 classrooms and teacher-education programs. For example, the studies highlight the voice of a girl who says she has dreams and goals and wants to be challenged, the voice of a boy who says the more his parents can be involved the better outcomes he will have, and the voices of many young students who say their cultural backgrounds matter and are an integral part of who they are and how they experience school.

Likewise, the perceptions of preservice teachers allow teacher educators insight into their experiences. Key to closing the lingering achievement gap is to have informed teachers in the workforce who understand how to teach and support children from all backgrounds. Recruiting and retaining teachers who represent the student population and who are culturally responsive remain crucial needs.

Through taking the time to create your own cultural autobiography and sharing your story with colleagues, family, or friends, you will take the first step in examining your cultural lens, or the way in which you view the world around you. This is the lens through which you make sense of people's actions, decisions, and ways of life. You begin to see how this informs your philosophy of teaching, the instructional decisions you make, and the approaches to classroom management and discipline you take.

Until more individuals of diversity in race, ethnicity, and culture enter the teaching profession, which is one means to combat cultural mismatch, current and preservice teachers must work to better understand the cultural background of their students and how those unique beliefs and experiences that make up their cultural background contribute to the process of educating them. In my framework for overcoming cultural mismatch, educational professionals will become aware of key mechanisms that lead to building more inclusive schools.

This book serves to provide readers with the necessary background knowledge on cultural mismatch and how to overcome its barriers. What may seem like broad themes are introduced, but these are presented in a relevant and accessible way in the framework so that teachers and school leaders can begin the journey toward culturally responsive teaching. I hope that every stakeholder reading this book realizes that while the process of becoming a culturally responsive teacher takes time and requires a shift in thinking, getting started with the process of introspection is a useful first step to which all school professionals should commit.

~

Acknowledgments

To my husband: To realize the roles of wife of eleven years, mother of two, university professor, and author is because you are such a gracious best friend. Thank you, and I will always love you.

To my children: If you hadn't been building forts, riding your scooters a lot, and playing in the backyard, this book would have never come to fruition. For that, I am truly grateful. You inspire me, I love you, and this book is dedicated to you.

To my parents: Your sacrifices to see your children succeed in life will never be forgotten. I owe you everything. You are deeply loved.

To all my great teachers and mentors: Thank you all for your support and generosity. May all young people have someone like you in their lives.

Introduction

Students in U.S. public schools represent an array of cultural heritages. From students' cultures emerge different ways of constructing knowledge, making sense of experiences, and learning (Gay, 2000). The majority of American teachers, unlike their students, are white, monocultural females who lack experience with individuals of other cultures. Student diversity in U.S. schools is increasing at a faster rate than teachers of color. As a result there is a cultural mismatch between students and those entrusted to be their teachers.

How will these teachers reach students who differ from them culturally, and are they ready, willing, and able to do so? The differences in cultural backgrounds between teachers and students in America's schools can present difficulty for teachers particularly in knowing how to learn about students' diverse backgrounds and how to utilize facets of those cultures to inform the teaching and learning process. The result is that teachers have difficulty effectively educating students of diverse cultures, managing the classroom, engaging students, handling communication, and incorporating background knowledge and learning styles.

This book introduces readers to the theory, research, and implications of cultural mismatch. Two mechanisms for activating change are presented in this book: a framework for overcoming cultural mismatch and an inclusive schools action plan. Stirring up a sense of urgency in educators and then guiding school teams on planning, implementation, and measurement, teachers and school leaders can commit now to embracing diversity.

If teachers do not proportionally represent the racial, cultural, and ethnic composition of the students they serve, educators must integrate culturally responsive practices in daily instruction in order to cultivate learning and guide student achievement. Teachers must be ever mindful of the knowledge and understanding students bring with them to the classroom. They must be equipped to use familiar cultural information and processes to scaffold learning for students, focusing on "relationships, cognitive scaffolding, and critical social awareness" (Hammond, 2015, p. 156).

Wong (2008) points to the changing demographics in the United States and the need for teachers who can understand and relate to their students. Unless teachers can respond to students' cultures and use their backgrounds as springboards for learning, their achievement will be stifled. Even teachers of color and teachers who have experienced a rich cultural upbringing may not be fully aware of how to utilize culturally responsive teaching practices. So all educators should unite and include and support diversity together.

Even prior to 2011, numbers of racially and ethnically diverse students were already on the rise. According to the National Center for Education Statistics (2011), "between 1990 and 2010, the percentage of public school students who were white decreased from 67 to 54 percent, and the percentage of those who were Hispanic increased from 12 percent (5.1 million students) to 23 percent (12.1 million students)" (p. 26). In 2009, more than 11 million school-age children in the United States spoke a language other than English, which is an increase of more than 6 million students (U.S. Department of Education, 2014). Given the continued growth in diversity of the student population served in U.S. schools, teachers and administrators must acquire the knowledge and skills to successfully educate students of all races, ethnicities and cultures. School leaders must also act to ensure that culturally responsive teaching practices are implemented in all classrooms.

To effectively teach all children—regardless of ethnic, racial, socioeconomic, religious, and other differences—the preservice teacher must also be aware of the role a student's cultural background plays in their readiness to learn and how they learn. To develop this awareness, the preservice teacher can reflect on his or her own cultural background and how it informs his or her teaching. Through creating a cultural autobiography, a springboard for continuous professional improvement and beginning to learn and practice culturally responsive teaching is founded.

If preservice teachers and practicing teachers alike know their own cultural lens, they will develop an understanding of the importance of cultural background in reaching and teaching their students. Hammond (2015) states, "Culture is like the air we breathe, permeating all we do. And the hardest culture to examine is often our own, because it shapes our actions in ways that seem invisible and normal" (p. 55). The description of the cultural autobiography process guides educators through an introspective journey.

Two cases are shared in this book that focus on exploring perceptions of teachers and students respectively. One case explores preservice teachers' perceptions of the process of creating a cultural autobiography during their preservice, university coursework as well as their perceptions of teaching diverse students. The other case explores students' perceptions of their teachers' culturally responsive teaching, which is triangulated with teacher and principal input.

The first study highlighted in this book is a multiple case study in which elementary school students, their teachers, and the school principals were interviewed. The study's purpose was to explore the perceptions students had about their teachers and how those compared to the tenets of culturally responsive teaching. The perceptions of students, teachers and school administrators were compiled and analyzed in the qualitative study.

The second study explored the voices of preservice teachers at a small, private university in the southeastern United States. It examined their personal experience with the cultural autobiography they created as an undergraduate course requirement as well as their beliefs on teaching diverse students. Preservice teachers created a cultural autobiography through self-reflection. They did this by responding to a number of questions related to beliefs and values, considering misconceptions and biases, and then sharing their answers in a discussion with peers.

A single case study was conducted with three preservice teachers once preliminary data was received from eight participants in the initial round of electronic questionnaires. Results showed strong value for the cultural autobiography process by preservice teachers. As schools continue to become increasingly diverse, and with cultural mismatch on the rise, the need for preservice teachers to be prepared to relate to and educate all students from all demographics has never been more important.

Using the background knowledge and experiences students take from their respective cultures, teachers can foster meaningful learning opportunities for students (Ladson-Billings, 1995; Gay, 2000; T. C. Howard, 2001). In the same way, preservice teachers should use their background as a foundation from which to learn and grow in specific areas, for example, cultural awareness and cultural competence. One of the first steps on the path to becoming a culturally responsive teacher is for the teacher to create a cultural autobiography, which initiates introspection.

The process of writing a cultural autobiography is included in the framework for overcoming cultural mismatch, which highlights action steps that are practical and provide guidance for schools to begin to implement culturally responsive teaching. Steps that must be taken by teachers include getting to know the cultural backgrounds of your students, getting to know your own cultural background through introspection and possible biases held that may affect teaching, and building partnerships with parents.

School administrators must support teachers in these action steps. Furthermore, they must require culturally responsive teaching practices, recruit and retain minority teachers, and build partnerships with families and community organizations. Additionally, an inclusive schools action plan should be written at every school by a site-based team representative of the student body and inclusive of school personnel, students, and parents. Recommendations for action plan activities, like surveying students and teachers and hosting a cultural autobiography symposium, are included in chapter 8.

~

CHAPTER ONE

Nowhere to Hide Part 1

Cultural Mismatch in U.S. Public Schools

Envision yourself in a room where you are different from others. Picture that you are different from every other person in the room. Maybe you look different, speak a different language, have different interests or beliefs, or have different abilities. Now picture yourself as a student in any pre-kindergarten through twelfth-grade classroom, different from everyone in the room, whether physically, mentally, socially, emotionally, culturally, or any other difference.

Some of those differences could be having brown skin unlike anyone else in the room, speaking another language better than English, or observing different religious beliefs and practices. Other differences in the school setting could include how students display respect versus how teachers perceive respectful behavior, how students communicate versus how teachers evaluate acceptable communication styles, and student engagement versus teachers' careful planning of instructional delivery based on students' needs.

Now imagine having no advocate in the classroom. You are left to assimilate and expected to score well on high-stake assessments though no interest in or inclusion of your cultural background is apparent. Who will help you feel a sense of belonging and thus a readiness to learn? Who sees value in who you already are? Who is willing to discover how your background can add to your school experience? Who really knows who you are without assuming they know who you are?

As an educator, teacher in training, or school leader, how will you advocate for every student in your classroom, giving them a sense of belonging and helping them reach their potential? Students must have a sense that despite differences, each of them is uniquely important in the classroom and has a purpose in the future. Instilling in students that their background is important to their achievement, the classroom community, and also their own learning is too often pushed aside. Teachers are either unaware or over- look that students' cultural backgrounds can be used as a catalyst for positive student outcomes.

People gravitate toward and feel that they fit in with other people they can relate to and with whom they share similarities. These similarities may be common interests, spoken language, nationality, religion, shared experi- ences, culture, and more. From these personal connections, relationships are founded and fostered. Through relationships, individuals best accomplish goals and solve problems. This is no different in the school setting where teachers must form relationships with students in light of the disproportion- ality of their racial or cultural background compared to that of their students.

Carver-Thomas (2018) states that for black students the "benefit of having a black teacher for just 1 year in elementary school can persist over several years, especially for black students from low-income families" (p. 4). This results in positive outcomes for black students academically but also socially and emotionally. Matching minority students to minority teachers, while limited due to teachers of color being only 20 percent of the work- force, can have the following benefits: stereotypes are lessened, the teacher may serve as a more effective role model, and the students are more likely to graduate high school and excel in college (Carver-Thomas, 2018).

Individuals considering a career in teaching must be aware of and truly understand the needs of today's students. Teachers should not simply transfer their own perspectives from their schooling experiences and perceptions of how students learn to their students. The teacher should not assume that his or her perspective is the same as the student's. Accordingly, the teacher must realize the need for confronting bias and assumptions. Current or preservice teachers are misguided if they believe they will know how to teach or know how students learn based on their own experiences in school.

This thinking is common yet very detrimental to building positive rela- tionships with students and reaching desired academic goals in the class- room. Dana and Yendol-Hoppey (2020) state,

> The famous quote attributed to Anais Nin, "We don't see things as they are, we see things as we are," is helpful to understand why reading to appreciate our own and others' perspectives is important to the work of a teacher researcher,

particularly related to groups of students that are not equitably served by the current schooling system. (p. 78)

Teachers must think of their students as the "consumers." They must get to know that target audience and be prepared to meet students' needs by tapping in to their abilities, interests, and background knowledge. Student differences exist in academic ability, socioeconomic status, racial or ethnic identity, learning style, motivation, and more. A year with students is the teacher's opportunity to take students from their current level of knowledge and ability to their potential for that year. This is done through creating strong bonds and a culture of care and tapping in to the perspectives and cultural backgrounds of the students.

This chapter focuses on the cultural mismatch that exists between teachers and students in U.S. public schools. Teachers, school administrators, district level administrators, and all stakeholders are encouraged to gain awareness and knowledge of cultural mismatch, its negative effects as well as the beauty that can come from focusing on inclusion. Informing teachers and school personnel of the effects of cultural mismatch is the first step to energizing them to overcome its barriers. The goal is to lead underrepresented students to success in the nation's schools by harnessing the unique abilities, talents, and interests of those students.

Cultural mismatch is defined by difference in race, ethnicity, or culture between the teacher and student. Classroom settings may have many, just a few, or even only one example of cultural mismatch between the teacher and students. In some schools, the entire classroom of students may differ greatly in cultural background from the teacher. Every scenario presents a divide and a more difficult time in relationship-building; therefore, the teacher must create a setting in which understanding the students' differences must be planned for, implemented, and then reflected upon.

With a disparity of racially and ethnically diverse teachers, the vast majority of teachers in the United States are white and monolingual. The number of black and Native American teachers is on the decline (Carver-Thomas, 2018). Drawing attention to these changing demographics, Davis (2012) states, "We can't deny that our children are changing in complexion and complexity, and you may find yearly more children in your classroom who don't look like you or each other" (p. 6).

Evidenced by the percentage of Hispanic teachers at only 8.8 percent in 2015–2016, the "gap between the percentage of Latinx teachers and students is larger than for any other racial or ethnic group" (Carver-Thomas, 2018, p. 2). Until more minority individuals pursue and begin a career in teaching, current classroom teachers must become aware of what cultural mismatch is and how it can hinder student learning and development if it is not properly identified and if measures for overcoming its barriers are not put in place.

According to the National Center for Education Statistics (2019), during the 2017–2018 school year 79.3 percent of public school teachers, elementary and secondary combined, were white. This decreased by 5 percent after 1999–2000. Yet, the percentage of white students in schools decreased by 12 percent, from 61 to 49 percent. The number of white students in public schools is expected to decrease further to 45 percent by the fall of 2027.

Of minority teacher demographics, 6.7 percent were black, 9.3 percent were Hispanic, 2.1 percent were Asian, Pacific Islander or American Indian/ Alaska Native combined and encompassed less than 1 percent of the teaching force, and individuals of two or more races made up only 1.8 percent. Seventeen percent of the 47.2 million public school students in the fall of 2000 were black. This number decreased to 15 percent in the fall of 2015 and is expected to remain the same through the fall of 2027. Hispanic students composed 16 percent in the fall of 2000, with an increase to 26 percent in the fall of 2015. This population of students is expected to grow to 29 percent by the fall of 2027 (National Center for Education Statistics, 2019).

In 2010, 47 percent of students in the southern United States were white, but by 2015, black and Hispanic students combined at 48 percent to become the majority in public schools. In the western United States, Hispanic students became the majority in 2015 at 42 percent of the population from 41 percent white in 2010; however, in the Northeast and Midwest, white students still make up the majority of students in public schools (National Center for Education Statistics, 2019).

The cultural mismatch in city schools is significant. During the 2015–2016 school year, 69 percent of teachers working at city schools were white while the other 31 percent were minorities comprised of any race or ethnicity other than white. Schools with 90 percent or more minority students were noted to have a teaching force with 45 percent white teachers while schools with between 75 and 89 percent minority students had a teaching staff of 69 percent white teachers. In schools of 50 to 74 percent minority students, 80 percent of the teachers were white (National Center for Education Statistics, 2019).

Data on cultural mismatch also includes school settings with less than half of a minority student population and small populations of diverse students. In schools with 25 to 49 percent minority students, 90 percent of the teachers were white. While 96 percent of the teachers were white in schools with 10 to 24 percent minority composition, 98 percent of the teachers were white in school demographics less than 10 percent diverse. This mismatch can be very problematic for students who cannot relate to their teacher but also have fewer students like them in the school to relate to (National Center for Education Statistics, 2019).

All student race or ethnicity categories other than white are underrepresented when compared to that of teachers. As a result, the likelihood of a minority student having a teacher who shares his or her cultural background is unlikely. Students and teachers whose racial and ethnic backgrounds match favor a positive impact for student achievement as well as attitudes toward school and motivation, and minority teachers may hold minority students to higher expectations than white teachers (Egalite & Kisida, 2018; Egalite, Kisida, & Winters, 2015; Carver-Thomas, 2018).

Identifying cultural mismatch is the first step to noticing difference, learning about difference, and ultimately esteeming difference for the beauty that it is and the positive outcomes it can help foster. No longer is an "I don't see color. I just see students" attitude acceptable. This color-blind mentality leaves out the essence of who the student is and was created to be. Moreover, it gives an impression that the teacher is avoiding learning about difference. It also gives the impression that the teacher is not interested in and sees no value in including students' cultural influences in the classroom and school experience.

There are several steps the preservice teacher, practicing teacher, and school leader can take to learn about cultural mismatch and how to overcome its effects. Acquiring more information about your students than academic indicators alone is key. Considering your knowledge of the demographic composition of your students, studying and experiencing other cultures, and formally creating a cultural autobiography are some preliminary steps for beginning culturally responsive teaching. A framework for overcoming cultural mismatch is introduced in chapter 8 and provides further action steps.

Teachers are often required to gather all pertinent academic data from previous years about students prior to instructing them. This includes but is not limited to report cards, standardized assessments, and curriculum-based assessments. Reviewing documentation related to any health issues, special needs, or accommodations is also a role of the teacher in beginning a new school year. It is equally important to review student demographic information, like whether students receive free or reduced lunch or are classified as homeless.

Likewise, reviewing the racial or ethnic composition of the students and recognizing possible cultural mismatch is another crucial step in getting to know students. Teachers should take the time to learn about their students and to acknowledge and welcome difference. The extra time and effort put into knowing your student as a whole person and not just their academic portfolio results in fewer communication and discipline problems as the year goes on. A foundation for expectations, communication, and interaction is established.

After carefully reviewing student data, teachers should consider the following questions about themselves and their students.

- How are my students' racial or ethnic identities similar to and different from mine?
- What do I know about my students' racial or ethnic identities?
- How will I build relationships with students who are racially or ethnically different from me?
- How will I create opportunities to get to know my students' racial or ethnic identities?
- How will I get to know my students from their cultural perspectives?

Educating yourself is the next crucial activity for educators. You can become more informed about different races, cultures, and ethnicities through reading about them; taking a course at a local college or university; watching documentaries; attending diverse community events like festivals, fairs, and church services; volunteering in diverse communities or with diverse students; or signing up for a missions trip whether local, national, or international. Taking part in these types of personal growth activities prior to becoming a teacher is ideal; however, it is never too late to gain experience in culturally diverse settings.

Finally, participating in discourse with other people who have common interests in the advancement of underrepresented populations and the teaching of diverse students is important. Educators are called to ask and inquire about what they do not know. They can do this by asking families to share their backgrounds and cultures, asking students to complete an interest inventory form with questions about culture, holding a discussion with colleagues and students about similarities and differences, or completing and sharing a cultural autobiography. Students can also create their own cultural autobiographies.

Conclusion

"Cultural mismatch" refers to a teacher–student assignment in which the race, ethnicity, and culture of the teacher and the student differ. The term "cultural mismatch" has become more relevant as demographics continue to shift toward increased diversity across the country. Until more minority individuals pursue careers in teaching, cultural mismatch will remain, with its negative implications—including prejudice, bias, assumptions, and discrimination—for student achievement and social-emotional development if educators do not see themselves as agents of change to help overcome this injustice.

The difficulty does not lie in the differences between teachers and students but in how teachers respond to students in various school situations, like methods of instruction, classroom management, and student discipline practices. The differences students have should be welcomed and incorporated in the classroom. Teachers and school leaders can overcome cultural mismatch through beginning the journey of culturally responsive teaching.

This is done through teachers getting to know students beyond literacy and mathematics indicators. They should also commit to an introspective process considering their differences and the impact this may have on classroom instruction. The creation of a cultural autobiography is valuable to preserve teachers as well. It should be incorporated in their college or university teacher preparation program. All educators who have never taken part in the process, regardless of their years of experience, should participate. The cultural autobiography is further detailed in chapter 6, and mechanisms for overcoming cultural mismatch are discussed in chapter 8.

CHAPTER TWO

~

Nowhere to Hide Part 2

The Lingering Achievement Gap in U.S. Public Schools

Every child deserves a quality education that guides them toward career readiness. Preparing students academically so that they have many choices in postsecondary options should be the goal of educators and educational leaders. Students must be ready to compete in a global and ever-changing workforce. They will be our best and brightest tomorrow, coming from all racial and cultural backgrounds.

Students may face barriers out of their control like living in poverty, lack of parental support and resources, and factors related to learning English as a second language. Davis (2012) lists "poverty, academic course work, test bias, teacher expectations, and teacher quality" as some of the factors that schools can work to remedy (p. 98). Teachers can no longer just blame these factors and hold back students of diversity from reaching their individual potential and maximizing their future vocation options. The lingering student achievement gap must be confronted. The lack of inclusion of cultural influences can no longer be ignored.

This chapter will take a look at 2019 National Assessment of Education Progress (NAEP) data and other relevant data from previous years that illustrate significant differences in student scores when disaggregated by the racial/ethnic identity of students. Educational statistics are reported and analyzed in this specific area to determine the achievement of all students and to highlight the disparity in this particular nationwide assessment.

While schools have focused on a wide variety of academic initiatives, interventions, and programs tailored to improve academic achievement, focus should now be placed on improving the education experience of underrepresented students through incorporating their cultural identities and influences in classroom instruction. This diversity makes up America's public school student population, and it is time to know the student as a whole person, including his or her cultural perspective and voice.

Educators and educational leaders are setting themselves and their students up for failure when they do not consider students' cultural background and how this informs the teaching and learning process. Increased efforts must be put forth in solving this great deficit facing minority children. Overcoming cultural mismatch is a key element of the conversation on closing achievement gaps.

Ladson-Billings (2007) dispels the myths related to low achievement of African American minorities and children of poverty and points to the many factors related to the black–white student achievement gap. This brings to light the need for more discourse and a shift in thinking to move forward and raise the achievement of all students with a specific emphasis on students who continue to encounter school failure. A shift away from stereotypes and assumptions and a shift toward the positive role the teacher can play must occur.

Renewed emphasis should be placed on the student-teacher relationship with special consideration given to awareness of cultural mismatch and the negative classroom effects that may result. Edwards (2010) states, "It is well documented that achievement gaps exist and persist across not only race, but also income and place of residency. These educational inequities deny millions of our children the opportunities to develop their unique abilities and gifts, to find personal success, and to achieve economic well-being" (p. 23).

Culturally responsive teaching, viewed as one answer to closing the achievement gap, has the potential to lessen the effects caused by the cultural mismatch of teachers and students in today's schools (Parhar & Sensoy, 2011). Because culturally responsive teaching can address poor achievement by minority students, researchers have advocated for its inclusion since the 1990s (Parhar & Sensoy, 2011).

Teachers must consider the effect on minority and low socioeconomic status students who are taught from a perspective that lacks diverse cultural viewpoints and emphasizes a middle-class, European framework (T. C. Howard, 2003). Their customs, traditions and values are ignored and they are forced to assimilate to the methodology of American schools (Gay, 2010). This adds an additional barrier to those that may already exist.

Researchers, educators, and concerned stakeholders are called to draw their focus to what really helps failing students succeed. Ladson-Billings

(2007) suggests turning from deficit thinking to empowering students. The focus is placed on what students can do and not what the research has historically shown they cannot do. G. Howard (2006) suggests examining the achievement gap through the lens of school improvement instead of placing blame on student differences and lack of parental involvement. These gaps in minority student achievement persist even when educational scores as a whole improve.

National Academic Performance of Public School Students

In 2019, the most recent administration of the NAEP was given to fourth-, eighth-, and twelfth-grade students. Gaps in academic achievement of black and Hispanic students compared to white students were still of great concern. These disparities have been lingering since the first administration of the assessment in 1992. This section presents student performance outcomes for the achievement gap, with regard to the white–black and white–Hispanic achievement gaps and black enrollment density.

The student performance statistics in table 2.1 include the percentages of students who scored at or above the NAEP proficient level. The proficient level represents student academic performance and competency over challenging subject matter at the designated grade level, including subject-matter knowledge, application of such knowledge to real-world situations, and analytical skills appropriate to the subject matter (National Center for Education Statistics, 2019).

National Data on U.S. Lingering Achievement Gaps
In 2011 the Nation's Report Card—the official results report of student performance on the NAEP—included two specific reports on existing achievement gaps in U.S. schools. These included the Black–White Gaps Report and the Hispanic–White Gaps Report in which the progress of fourth- and eighth-grade students in the specific race category was reported for reading, mathematics, and science in the five most populous states: Florida, Texas, California, New York, and Illinois. White students outperformed all other subgroups except Asian/Pacific Islander on the 2011 fourth- and eighth-grade reading and mathematics assessments. These results remain true for the most recent assessment results.

From 2003 to 2019, the fourth-grade NAEP mathematics assessments showed white–black gap scores ranging from 24 to 27. Racial/ethnic gap scores are provided to compare the achievement of underrepresented groups to that of white students. A gap score appears when one subgroup of students outper-

Table 2.1.   Percentage of Students Scoring at or above the NAEP Proficient Level

Racial/Ethnic Identity	4th Grade Math (2019)	4th Grade Reading (2019)	8th Grade Math (2019)	8th Grade Reading (2019)	12th Grade Math (2015)	12th Grade Reading (2015)
Overall	41	35	34	34	25	37
White	52	45	44	42	32	46
Black	20	18	14	15	7	17
Hispanic	28	23	20	22	12	25
Asian/Pacific Islander	66	55	62	54	46	48
Asian	69	57	64	57	47	49
Native Hawaiian/Other Pacific Islander	28	25	21	25	Included in Asian/Pacific Islander	Included in Asian/Pacific Islander
American Indian/Alaska Native	24	19	15	19	10	28
Two or More Races	44	40	38	37	31	45

Source: National Assessment of Educational Progress (2019)

forms another. The score is the difference between the average scale scores of each subgroup. Gap scores provide statistical information for educators, school leaders, and policymakers to understand achievement discrepancy and inform decision making related to school improvement planning initiatives.

The Black–White Achievement Gap

From 1990 to 2000, higher gap scores from 31 to 35 are noted. During the last seven administrations of the eighth-grade NAEP mathematics from 2007 to 2019, the score gap between white and black students toggled from 31 to 32, with the most recent 2019 gap score at 32. The gap score in 2005 was 35 and 34 in 2007. Prior to that, the gap score was as high as 39–41 between the years 1992 to 2000.

For the seven administrations of the fourth-grade NAEP reading assessments from 2007 to 2019, the white–black gap scores ranged from 25 to 27 with the gap score in 2019 remaining at 27. Higher gap scores of 30 to 34 were seen on the five administrations between the years 1998 to 2003. The 1998 administration saw the highest gap score of 38. On the eighth-grade NAEP reading assessment in 2019, the white–black gap score was 28, which was the highest it had been since the administration in 2005. Between those years on six administrations, the gap score ranged from 25 to 27. The highest gap scores reported were 30 in 1992 and 1994.

The Hispanic–White Achievement Gap

The achievement gap between white and Hispanic students on both the fourth- and eighth-grade administrations of the reading and mathematics assessments did not improve even though some gains were made in overall scores for certain grades and subjects. On the fourth-grade NAEP mathematics assessment, the white–Hispanic gap score during the four administrations of 2013 to 2019 ranged from 18 to 19. From 2003 to 2011, the gap scores were slightly higher, ranging from 20 to 22. From 1992 to 2000, the gap scores ranged from 25 to 27 on four administrations. In 2009, eleven states had a narrower achievement gap than the nation, and two states—Rhode Island and Texas—had a wider gap (Hemphill & Vanneman, 2011).

The gap score between white and Hispanic assessment participants on the eighth-grade NAEP mathematics in 2017 and 2019 was 24. From 1996 until 2015, there was steady decrease from the gap score of 30 in 1996 to the score of 22 in 2015, except for the 2000 administration, when the gap score increased by 1. For the 2009 administration, seven states demonstrated student performance that narrowed the white–Hispanic achievement gap, with two states—Arkansas and Delaware—demonstrating overall higher performance by Hispanic students than white students. Two states—Maryland and Utah—had a wider gap, with increases in overall higher performance of white students (Hemphill & Vanneman, 2011).

The white–Hispanic gap score for the 2019 administration of the fourth-grade reading NAEP was at its lowest with a score of 21; however, in the seven prior administrations between the years 2005 to 2017, the gap scores ranged from 23 to 26. In 2002 and 2003, the gap scores were 28. In both 1994 and 2000, the gap scores were at 35. For the 2009 administration, the achievement gap between white and Hispanic students in New York and New Jersey narrowed as the overall performance of Hispanic students improved compared to white students. The states of Colorado and Indiana experienced widening gaps (Hemphill & Vanneman, 2011).

Between the years 2003 and 2017, the gap scores of white and Hispanic students on the eighth-grade NAEP reading assessment steadily decreased from 27 to 19, with an increase to 20 on the 2019 administration. Prior to that and dating back to 1992, a range from 24 to 27 was reported. In 2009, the achievement gap was narrower than the national gap score in seven states (Hemphill & Vanneman, 2011).

Black Student Enrollment Density Report

The national data also included a look at the black enrollment density of schools, or the percentage of students in a school who are black. Black density enrollment further illustrates the threat of cultural mismatch. In the United States, black students on average attend schools with 48 percent or higher black student enrollment while white students on average attend schools with 9 percent black student enrollment. Black enrollment density is also simply referred to as "density" (Bohrnstedt et al., 2015).

Looking both across schools and within schools provides additional context for understanding the achievement gap. Seventy-seven percent of public schools in the United States have a density of 0 to 20 percent, so nearly 80 percent of schools have less than 20 percent black enrollment. Meanwhile, only 10 percent of schools fall into the 60 to 100 percent density range. This is one reason why school leaders for far too long have been able to avoid addressing the needs of marginalized students, such as black students, who make up such small percentages of the student body (Bohrnstedt et al., 2015).

The report included an analysis of the achievement of black and white students on the eighth-grade NAEP mathematics administration in 2011. In schools that had 60 to 100 percent density, the achievement gap between white and black students was greater, with black achievement being lower, while the achievement of white students was not significantly different from that of white students in less dense schools. Additionally, the achievement gap was wider in schools with 20 to 100 percent density than that of schools in the lowest reporting category with only 0–19 percent black enrollment density (Bohrnstedt et al., 2015).

Black enrollment density data can be further disaggregated as it varies by region. Sixty-seven percent of schools within the highest density category—60 to 100 percent—are city schools, and 47 percent of schools within the 40 to 60 percent density category are city schools. In the northwestern and midwestern United States combined, 84 percent of the densest schools are city schools whereas in the southern United States, 49 percent of the densest schools are city schools.

The south accounts for 46 percent of the highest density category. In fact, the south had the greatest numbers of schools in all density categories except 0–20 percent. For that category the west had the most schools with the lowest density student population (Bohrnstedt et al., 2015). These national indicators illustrate just how crucial it is for school leaders and teachers to get to know the specific students in their schools. While there are trends by region in the United States, critical analysis of state, district, and individual school demographics is needed to determine the level of cultural mismatch.

Numerous mechanisms have been identified in the research as factors that may contribute to lower achievement among black students. According to Bohrnstedt et al. (2015), additional factors that may affect black students include the following:

- less-experienced teachers and supports
- higher concentrations of families living in poverty, in single-family homes, and with parents with lower levels of education as well
- oppositional culture in which black students must overcome the fact that academic achievement can be seen as "acting white"
- teachers who hold lower expectations for black students
- academic tracking that begins as early as the elementary school years
- low-track tracking for black students in lower-density schools
- an increase in number of school discipline referrals as the number of black students increases

National Public School Discipline Data

This section presents an analysis of student discipline data in U.S. public schools. Data reported from the 2013–2014 school year provided national

Table 2.2. 2013–2014 Discipline Data by Percentage of Students by Race/Ethnicity

	In-School Suspension	One Out-of-School Suspension	More Than One Out-of-School Suspension	Expulsions	School-Related Arrests	Total Enrollment of Subgroup
White	39	35.1	28.9	45.3	33.4	50.4
Black	32.4	36.3	46	30.9	34.8	15.5
Hispanic	23.3	22.5	19.8	16.8	25.2	24.8
Asian	1.0	1.3	0.7	0.7	1.2	4.8
American Indian/Alaska Native	1.3	1.4	1.3	1.8	1.5	1.1
Native Hawaiian/Other Pacific Islander	0.2	0.4	0.3	0.2	0.8	0.4
Two or More Races	2.8	3.0	3.0	4.2	2.8	3.0

Source: U.S. Department of Education (2014)

discipline information for pre-K through twelfth-grade public schools (U.S. Department of Education, 2014). Many categories of discipline are included such as corporal punishment, suspension, arrest, and expulsion. The following categories are reported in table 2.2 with the percentage of students from each racial/ethnic subgroup identified: in-school suspension; one out-of-school suspension; more than one out-of-school suspension; expulsion; and school-related arrest.

Disproportionate discipline by race/ethnicity accounts for the most crippling effect of cultural mismatch. The percentage of students receiving disciplinary action in all subgroups except black students was lower than the percentage of total enrollment of the subgroup. While black students represent 15 percent of the public school population, black students received 32.4 percent of in-school suspensions, 36.3 percent of one out-of-school suspension, 46 percent of more than one out-of-school suspension, 30.9 percent of expulsions, and 34.8 percent of school-related arrest. These figures are between double and triple the percentage of black student enrollment (U.S. Department of Education, 2014).

Conclusion

The increasing racial and ethnic diversity within schools and the resulting significant cultural mismatch of teachers and students should ignite a sense of urgency in teachers and school leaders. Even when educational scores improve as a whole, a gap in the achievement of white and minority students remains (Barton & Coley, 2010).

Analyzing the data related to achievement gaps is meant to aid educators and decision makers in understanding this great barrier. Student achievement of underrepresented populations lags sorely behind that of white students. Paramount to overcoming this disproportionality is to discover the trends in student subgroup data, the needs of specific students on local and curriculum-based assessments, and strategies to engage students' cultures in the teaching and learning process. Designing instruction to meet those needs is the desired goal.

Teachers and administrators must not view students' school experiences through their own cultural lens but be equipped to teach students of all races, ethnicities, and cultures through culturally responsive teaching practices. The demographics of U.S. students are shifting rapidly so teachers must find ways to relate to students of different cultural backgrounds (Wong, 2008). They must respond to students' cultures and incorporate their backgrounds into their learning opportunities.

CHAPTER THREE

~

The Skinny on Culturally Responsive Teaching

Culture is defined as the "set of practices and beliefs shared by members of a particular group that distinguish that group from other groups" (Terrell, Robins, & Lindsey, 2009, p. 16). Culture refers to more than just the beliefs and customs of a certain group. When a person refers to his or her culture, he or she takes into account age, gender, socioeconomic status, geography, nationality, ethnicity, ancestry, religion, language, history, sexual orientation, physical and mental ability, occupation, and other characteristics.

Everything about a person weaves together to form the fabric of his or her culture. Davis (2012) describes culture as "the total of everything an individual learns by growing up in a particular context and results in a set of expectations for appropriate behavior in seemingly similar contexts" (p. 7). Culture serves as a frame of reference that a person uses subconsciously when understanding experiences, interpreting events, making connections to process new information, and making decisions.

This frame of reference forms a lens through which a person sees and responds to experiences and circumstances around them. Davis (2012) states, "Think of it as a pair of glasses that allow you to see the world differently from every other person who inhabits it" (p. 7). This can inform basic things like food choices, interacting with other people, and daily schedules and activities, but this can also inform more significant things like vocation choice, religious beliefs and practices, social and emotional characteristics, communication style, and more.

A person's culture also informs the decisions he or she makes and the reasoning behind the decision making. Examples of cultural backgrounds informing decision making for teachers include how and when discipline is applied in the classroom, how communication is handled, and whether or not teachers choose to provide students with a platform where their voices are heard. Regarding students, their cultural background influences whom they socialize with, how they approach schoolwork, how they interact with the teacher, whether they display emotion or bottle it up, and so on.

While cultural influences may be subtle or even unknown to some, for others they are the simple features that make up daily life. Chavez and Guido-DiBrito (1999) assert that individuals from minority populations define race and culture in a very conscious way due to cultural and social influences. The authors identify two ways that race and culture are constructed, and these two actually work each in conflict with the other.

> First, deep conscious immersion into cultural traditions and values through religious, familial, neighborhood, and educational communities instills a positive sense of ethnic identity and confidence. Second, and in contrast, individuals often must filter ethnic identity through negative treatment and media messages received from others because of their race and ethnicity. (p. 39)

This is a contrast to the racial identity construction of individuals who are white. Their enculturation is seen as unconscious because "their societal norms have been constructed around their racial, ethnic, and cultural frameworks, values, and priorities and then referred to as 'standard American culture' rather than as 'ethnic identity'" (Chavez & Guido-DiBrito, 1999, p. 39). Racial and cultural identity development is a progression that moves from the unconscious to the conscious. Ethnic identity is established through shared culture, language, religion, traditions, celebrations, and beliefs.

No one is free of culture. Individuals must look inward to tap into and discover their culture if it is not already familiar to them. The beauty, differences, and similarities that lay within an individual's unique culture and make them who they are must first be understood personally before we can understand how it informs teaching and decision making in the school setting. This chapter presents the literature on culturally responsive teaching and provides implications for classroom implementation.

Culturally Responsive Teaching Defined

In the literature on culturally responsive teaching, several frameworks and a variety of terminologies exist such as "culturally relevant; responsive, congruent, or sensitive pedagogy; teaching; instruction; multicultural education; and equity pedagogy, among others" (Morrison, Robins, & Rose, 2008, p. 434). In table 3.1, the most prominent researchers in the field and their specific terms with slightly different explanations are listed.

Under the multicultural pedagogy umbrella, culturally responsive teaching centers on the premise that "students' experiences, cultural connections, learning styles, and backgrounds are strengths rather than deficits and can be used to shore up academic achievement, school and classroom community, and students' human value, intellectual capacity, and performance responsibilities" (Moore, 2007, p. 28).

Culturally responsive teaching is a product of and a complementary approach to the field of multicultural education (Moore, 2007). Multicultural education is intended to transform the school so that students from diverse backgrounds are treated equally in all aspects of school life (Gay, 2000). This includes academic and social and emotional components and also relates to how students are disciplined. Multicultural education provides a platform for equality, and culturally responsive teaching facilitates active inclusion of students' unique backgrounds in their learning.

A culturally responsive classroom exudes care and concern for the student. It centers on the student, not the teacher, and supports the cultures of the learners. Students' unique strengths are identified, cultivated, and used to foster success in schools (Moore, 2007). Furthermore, students' respective identities, strengths, and weaknesses, unique languages, religious values, and different ethnicities are acknowledged as positive attributes. Individuality is nurtured; the differences of each child are celebrated and used as building blocks to success. The advantage of this design is that it "facilitates and supports the achievement of all students" (p. 28).

Various researchers have arrived at their own definition of cultural responsiveness as it pertains to education. Gay (2002) defines culturally responsive teaching as "using the cultural characteristics, experiences, and perspectives of ethnically diverse students as conduits for teaching them more effectively" (p. 106). Ladson-Billings (1995) uses "culturally relevant pedagogy" as somewhat synonymous to "culturally responsive teaching" and sees it as a framework for fostering student achievement, building cultural competence, and teaching students to identify and combat the inequities in society and schools.

When teachers welcome students' cultural insights and are not critical of them, they are facilitating culturally responsive practices in their classrooms (Brown-Jeffy & Cooper, 2011). Another sign of culturally responsive teaching is education made relevant to students because teachers have elicited

Table 3.1.   Major Authors on Cultural Responsiveness in Schools

Author	Term	Definition/Summary
Gay (2002)	Culturally responsive teaching	"Using the cultural characteristics, experiences, and perspectives of ethnically diverse students as conduits for teaching them more effectively" (p. 106).
		Diverse students will achieve better when their instruction is designed with their lived experiences and cultural frames of reference in mind. Five elements required of practitioners of culturally responsive teaching include developing a knowledge base about cultural diversity, including ethnic and cultural diversity content in the curriculum, demonstrating caring and building learning communities, communicating with ethnically diverse students, and responding to ethnic diversity in the delivery of instruction.
Howard, T. C. (2001)	Culturally responsive pedagogy	Culturally responsive pedagogy is "situated in a framework that recognizes the rich and varied cultural wealth, knowledge, and skills that students from diverse groups bring to schools, and seeks to develop dynamic teaching practices, multicultural content, multiple means of assessment, and a philosophical view of teaching that is dedicated to nurturing student academic, social, emotional, cultural, psychological, and physiological well-being" (pp. 67–68).
		This framework "embodies a professional, political, cultural, ethical, and ideological disposition" (p. 67) when addressing school success for diverse students.
Ladson-Billings (1995)	Culturally relevant pedagogy	Culturally responsive pedagogy rests on three criteria: (1) students must experience academic success; (2) students must develop and maintain cultural competence; and (3) students must develop a critical consciousness through which they challenge the status quo of the social order.
		Culturally responsive pedagogy is a framework for fostering student achievement, building cultural competence, and teaching students to identify and combat inequities in society and schools. It is a way for teachers and schools to value and draw upon the cultural make up of students and tie them into the teaching and learning process.

Author	Term	Definition/Summary
Brown-Jeffy & Cooper (2011)	Principles of culturally relevant pedagogy	Identity and achievement—identity development, cultural heritage, multiple perspectives, affirmation of diversity, and public validation of home-community cultures that includes the social and cultural capital that students bring to school with them. Equity and excellence—dispositions, incorporation of multicultural curriculum content, equal access, and high expectations. Developmental appropriateness—learning styles, teaching styles, and cultural variation in psychological needs (motivation, morale, engagement, collaboration). Teaching the whole child—skill development in a cultural context, home-school-community collaboration, learning outcomes, supportive learning community, and empowerment. Student–teacher relationships—caring, relationships, interaction, and classroom atmosphere.

students' cultural perspectives (Shealey & Callins, 2007). Hammond (2015) urges educators to think of culturally responsive teaching as "a mindset, a way of looking at the world" (p. 52). In this way, educators are urged to move away from a set of steps to follow and think more of a shift in thinking.

Ladson-Billings (1995) develops a theoretical framework for culturally relevant pedagogy. Within this framework, teachers who engage in culturally relevant pedagogy exhibit high academic expectations for students, demonstrate cultural competence, enable their students' cultural competency, and remain aware of social inequities in schools. Through analyzing the interviews, observations, and group analysis of videotaped classroom instruction, Ladson-Billings was able to formulate her theory of culturally relevant pedagogy.

Taking into account these data points, Ladson-Billings arrived at her theory. Specific criteria of culturally relevant pedagogy were formed. These include "an ability to develop students academically, a willingness to nurture and support cultural competence, and the development of a sociopolitical or critical consciousness" (p. 483). Using students' cultural influences in instruction is key as well as a commitment to a shift in thinking about the education of marginalized students.

T. C. Howard (2003) suggests that culturally relevant teaching will only work if teachers avoid making judgments based on perceptions of race and culture. Instead they should "develop individual profiles of students based on students' own thoughts and behaviors" (p. 201). He adds that previous attempts by schools have failed to meet the academic needs of diverse learners and that the key to effective pedagogy in incorporating students' cultural backgrounds must be founded on teachers' critical reflections.

Many researchers agree that the cultures of students are being ignored when students are forced to assimilate to a middle-class, European framework (Gay, 2010; T. C. Howard, 2003). Using a culturally responsive approach with culturally diverse students enables teachers to welcome students' cultural insights (Brown-Jeffy & Cooper, 2011). This is a required beginning step of culturally responsive teaching, yet fully including students' cultural backgrounds goes well beyond acknowledging and welcoming diversity.

Parhar and Sensoy (2011) define culturally responsive teaching as a practice that "recognizes students' differences, validates students' cultures, and asserts that upon cultural congruence of classroom practices, students will discover increasing success in school" (pp. 191–92). This approach asserts the value of focusing classroom curricula and practice upon students' cultural frames of reference. The authors suggest that when teachers have developed carefully designed lessons that allow students to construct their own meanings, they are met with academic success.

Cultural responsiveness is achieved when the construction of knowledge is embedded in a framework that requires students to draw upon their known cultural experiences. For example, student engagement is part of good teaching practices; however, components of student engagement—such as interesting activities, hands-on learning experiences, and deliberate planning of interactive lessons—are aspects of the preferred learning style in certain cultures (Gay, 2000).

Using such techniques not only provides students with the opportunity to "demonstrate what they know," but also affirms that "teaching and learning are more than cognitive and technical tasks" (Gay, 2000, p. 197). Students' social and emotional characteristics are also incorporated as these spring from the student's background and how they perceive the world and their school and classroom environment. Teachers who are culturally responsive see the benefit of creating a classroom in which students' respective backgrounds are integral in helping them make sense of new material (Villegas & Lucas, 2002).

Furthermore, these teachers exhibit a "high degree of sociocultural consciousness, hold affirming views of students of diverse backgrounds, see themselves as agents of change, understand and embrace constructivist views of learning and teaching, and know the students in their classes" (Villegas &

Lucas, 2002, p. 28). Classroom teachers who understand and value the role cultural background plays in students' respective schooling are more willing to listen to students. They are also more willing to include students' voices in teaching and classroom management, considering them to be important as active in their own learning experience.

Culturally responsive teaching is a way to raise the achievement of all students but especially that of minority groups, who have long been expected to conform to America's Eurocentric school system (Gay, 2000). T. C. Howard (2003) suggests that culturally responsive teaching may improve student achievement by creating lessons that include strands of students' own cultural identities and realities. Relevance and engagement ensue when students are able to relate to the content.

Teaching that aligns the entire education process to a framework that features students' cultural backgrounds is authentically culturally responsive. Specifically, communication, teaching, and learning styles and construction of knowledge must all be aligned with students' cultural implications. To accomplish this goal, school leaders and teachers must learn about their students and their various cultures (T. C. Howard, 2001).

Teachers who are culturally responsive display certain characteristics across the pedagogy (Siwatu, 2007). Such teachers embed culturally responsive practices in curriculum and instruction, classroom management, student assessment, and cultural enrichment and competence. Culturally responsive teachers also provide "students with the knowledge and skills needed to function in mainstream culture while simultaneously helping students maintain their cultural identity, native language, and connection to their culture" (Siwatu, 2007, pp. 1,086–87).

Making Culturally Responsive Teaching Happen

Sleeter (2011) argues that cultural responsiveness is understood only superficially and that basic conceptions about it mask the necessity of meaningful change regarding the framework through which teachers provide high quality, culturally sensitive learning opportunities. Teachers and school leaders need practical steps for activating this shift in thinking and instruction. This section provides information on how to implement culturally responsive teaching in the classroom.

Instruction that is culturally responsive should demonstrably incorporate facets of the student's total being: his or her prior experiences, racial and ethnic identity, and cultural and community experiences (Gay, 2010). Villegas and Lucas (2002) present the main characteristics of culturally responsive teaching and focus their work on preparing preservice teachers to begin their careers as effective culturally responsive teachers.

> Such a teacher a) is socioculturally conscious, that is, recognizes that there are multiple ways of perceiving reality and that these ways are influenced by one's location in the social order; b) has affirming views of students from diverse backgrounds, seeing resources for learning in all students rather than viewing differences as problems to be overcome; c) sees himself or herself as both responsible for and capable of bringing about educational change that will make schools more responsive to all students; d) understands how learners construct knowledge and is capable of promoting learners' knowledge construction; e) knows about the lives of his or her students; and f) uses his or her knowledge about students' lives to design instruction that builds on what they already know while stretching them beyond the familiar. (p. 21)

Sleeter (2011) proposes four areas in which professionals display limited knowledge: "cultural celebration, trivialisation, essentialising culture, and substituting cultural for political analysis of inequalities" (p. 12). The problem with cultural celebration is that teachers separate culture from academic study. This approach contrasts with culturally responsive teaching, which promotes academic achievement and development while affirming the cultural identity of students.

Unfortunately, cultures of diverse students are frequently only celebrated rather than used in the teaching and learning process to support student learning and development. Sleeter (2011) sees culturally relevant pedagogy being trivialized when school personnel attempt to simplify it with tools like checklists for practices that are culturally sensitive and lesson plans that include some multicultural elements. While a cultural diversity fair or cultural foods celebration may be enjoyed by the school community, true cultural responsiveness requires a much deeper analysis and commitment to marginalized students.

Essentializing race, culture, or ethnicity also compromises educators' ability to respond to diverse student populations. Sleeter (2011) defines "essentialising" as assuming commonalities within races, cultures, or ethnicities that limit educators' ability to tap into each student's individuality. Teachers must get to know students on an individual basis, and this includes getting to know their cultural background and their parents and family.

The opinions and perspectives of teachers directly impact their willingness, ability, and effectiveness in valuing and including the diverse backgrounds of all students. Teaching in this manner means choosing to support all students in the classroom, holding them to high standards, and planning rigorous lessons to facilitate learning and create engagement. Teachers must also display a willingness to learn and grow in their capacity to demonstrate cultural responsiveness. Moore (2007) presents a list of questions for reflection, asking teachers to reflect on their own practices as well as assess the student body they serve. The following questions are designed to help teachers assess their own cultural biases and prepare them for teaching diverse groups of students.

1) What support do the students need academically, socially, emotionally/mentally, and physically? 2) How will I prepare to effectively respond to these students and their needs? 3) What racial or cultural biases do I hold, and how will I keep them from influencing my teaching behaviors? 4) What resources (personnel and organizational) are available to assist me in being an efficacious culturally responsive educator? and finally 5) Am I culturally competent? (p. 28)

As teachers and school leaders reflect together on these questions, conversations about practicing cultural responsiveness pedagogy and improving student-teacher relationships will commence. Additionally, biases will emerge. Through creating a personal cultural autobiography, education professionals have a means to formally begin the introspective process required to begin the journey toward culturally responsive teaching. In subsequent chapters, the process for creating a cultural autobiography is introduced in more detail.

Every individual has some type of bias. This needs to be analyzed by the individual, and thought must be given to the effects of this bias. School personnel must become more informed to ultimately be able to reach and teach every child, regardless of their race, ethnicity, or culture. For all students to have a fulfilling school experience with academic success and social and emotional development, bias related to marginalized students must be acknowledged. Only then can teachers and administrators focus on ensuring high expectations for all students.

Conclusion

Practices that include and activate students' diverse backgrounds in the classroom environment are referred to slightly differently, but common characteristics exist. A main tenet of culturally responsive teaching is related to the teacher taking into account how students' cultural backgrounds inform their school experience and how they can aid students in personal achievement. Researchers look to culturally responsive teaching as a means to narrow the racial achievement gap.

Holding students to high expectations, facilitating parent involvement, respecting and empowering the voice of the individual, using cultural influences as a springboard for learning, and providing opportunities for students to share their culture are some of the characteristics of culturally responsive teaching. Teachers ought to build relationships with their students and seek to understand their respective cultural lenses. Students' cultural lenses affect how they view their world and their schooling experience. Getting to know each students' unique cultural influences aids teachers in deciding how to most effectively instruct them.

When culturally responsive teaching is employed, teachers make the decision to reduce threats of bias and stereotypes in the classroom. Their thinking contributes to student success. Deficit thinking, which includes seeing students as low achievers and focusing on student failures or even expecting them, remains unacceptable. Champions for marginalized students must continue to rally for their advocacy, breaking down this type of thinking and affording striving students opportunity through the power of culturally responsive teaching.

~

CHAPTER FOUR

More Than ABCs and 123s

Embracing Students' Cultural Diversity

An individual's culture is built upon his or her family upbringing and related life experiences. Some contributing factors include race, ethnicity, and religious beliefs. Other contributing factors include learned patterns of conduct in communication with others, socioeconomic influences providing or hindering basic needs, school experiences, perceived value of school, perceived value of work, nationality of parents or ancestors, languages spoken in the home, and celebrations.

Despite this, not everyone is aware of his or her culture. Consequently, he or she may not acknowledge the important role of cultural background and beliefs in a person's education and overall success. Influences of cultural background should not be ignored but included. Can students reach their potential without teachers actively knowing and tapping into the different cultures of their students? Teachers should not plan for rigorous, standards-based teaching and learning with great intentions yet without considering how students' backgrounds can aid the learning process.

Teachers should not treat their students as simply learners of a daily objective—rather, they must embrace the diversity of the whole child. Considering the social and emotional side of the child, teachers must take a step back and see the beauty that exists in each and every child. Students need the opportunity to have the whole of their existence—their culture—engaged. Getting to know students on an individual level is paramount. Teachers will not be able to reach and teach culturally diverse students without this connection. Positive relationships are crucial in the classroom but are especially vital for underrepresented students who may have experienced racism and social injustice in the past.

Academic content should be taught and learned within a setting that is culturally responsive and designed especially for the diverse group of students the teacher has in the classroom that year. From year to year the teacher must plan for and adjust instruction centered on the needs of the particular students. This is in contrast to teachers who use the same lesson plans year after year with no adjustments made and no regard for how students' cultural frames of reference can help support them in their own learning. This action leads one to believe that consideration of the specific students in the classroom is not important to pedagogy.

The classroom must first be a safe, orderly, and positive environment. A teacher's classroom management and organization must be well-designed and implemented, taking into account best practices as well as students' diverse cultural backgrounds. The implementation looks different in elementary schools compared to secondary settings, but common characteristics of a well-prepared teacher include teaching rules and procedures; setting high expectations for all students and holding them accountable; applying consequences and discipline consistently and fairly; and building trusting and caring relationships with all students.

Teachers with less experience working in urban settings with marginalized students must develop the skills necessary to manage a classroom and discipline students without assumptions and bias. It is crucial for preservice teachers to gain experience working with diverse students in schools that are working to narrow the racial achievement gap prior to completing their teacher-education program. Giving preservice teachers an opportunity to build meaningful relationships with students through getting to know them on a personal level allows them to begin to understand the experiences of diverse students.

This chapter focuses on the value of student perceptions in the educational setting. Listening to the student voice can give teachers a wealth of first-hand information about how their students perceive their own culture, how they think they learn best, their strengths and weaknesses, and their perception of their overall school experience. Teachers should not operate on an assumption of what they believe to be true about diverse students such as their learning style, communication style, cultural background, and so on. Directly eliciting this information from students removes the guesswork and provides valuable information about the student.

The Importance of Student Voice

Equally important to the pedagogical knowledge and skills of teachers and school leaders is student voice. This allows school professionals to obtain and consider direct accounts from students. Minimal data on student perception has been gathered despite the increasing amount of literature published on the need for and benefit of closing the achievement gap. If the cultural backgrounds of diverse students are to be used as the foundation on which learning is constructed and the experiences from which students make meaningful connections, it is necessary to elicit their beliefs and perceptions regarding cultural responsiveness in schools.

Decuir-Gunby, DeVance Taliaferro, and Greenfield (2010) elicited teachers' perceptions of the effectiveness of the American Excellence Association, which is a program for enhancing culturally relevant practices at the high school level and working to eliminate the racial achievement gap. Sixteen individuals from ten different high schools were interviewed. Focus group and individual interviews were conducted to collect data.

Themes that emerged included promoting African American academic achievement; creating a feeling of belonging and cultural competence; and developing critical consciousness through community service. Taking into consideration the limitations of the study, Decuir-Gunby, DeVance Taliaferro, and Greenfield (2010) state, "Most glaringly absent from this study were the voices of students" (p. 200). Taking into account the perceptions of teachers first, they propose further research that incorporates the perceptions of students.

Studying what students have to say about how teachers can draw from unique cultural backgrounds and experiences is vital. Educator practice in preparing annually for each new school year is lacking in acquiring student input and listening to the voices of students. This is important to glean ways in which students learn best and how they feel about their own experience and achievement in school. Along with schools' academic reform initiatives and interventions based on quantitative data analysis, school personnel should also be taking into account qualitative data by listening to input from students.

School leaders and teachers should become more aware of how students from culturally and linguistically diverse and low socioeconomic backgrounds feel about how they learn. In this way students, who best know their cultural background, can inform the curriculum, instruction, and classroom-management decisions of teachers. These mechanisms can include surveying the student body, conducting focus group interviews, and encouraging teachers to build personal relationships with students. Students also benefit from creating a cultural autobiography and sharing it with teachers and peers.

Eliciting beliefs and opinions provides talking points and allows dialogue to commence. A dialogue centered on personal cultural experiences provides a positive and inclusive setting in which to learn about others. All participants are given a platform to share their personal story. As a result, school leaders will have a glimpse of the beliefs and perspectives of students. That glimpse can improve school personnel respect and concern for students, willingness to include cultural background, and readiness to teach with high expectations for all students.

Student Voice in Research

Although limited research is available that investigates what students have to say about the inclusion of their respective cultures in the classroom setting, this section examines the ideas and opinions of students regarding culturally responsive practices in the educational setting. Teachers and school leaders should place great value on hearing from the voices of marginalized students. It also brings to light the call by researchers for more research incorporating the voice of the student.

The shortcomings of numerous interventions and misguided practices merit the creation of a space for students to offer potential solutions for what they believe works best for them in schools (T. C. Howard, 2001). In a study conducted during the 1997–1998 school year in a large elementary school in the northwestern United States in four classrooms of African American students, focus was placed on the students to "add to other efforts to put students' viewpoints, perceptions, and interpretations of their schooling experiences at the center of the discussion on school reform" (p. 132).

The study examined student input gathered from interviews and classroom observations from classes of culturally responsive teachers. The study included seventeen students of varying academic ability levels who were each interviewed individually and as part of a focus group. Through these interviews, T. C. Howard (2001) hoped to "understand their interpretation of the teaching practices and the extent to which the viewpoints were consistent with those of an outside observer and the teachers' intended goals and objectives" (p. 136).

Three themes emerged in the findings. The care of the teachers, family-style classroom atmospheres, and lively educational opportunities were recurring comments from students about their teachers and school experiences. T. C. Howard (2001) suggests that the students of culturally responsive teachers are able to note a difference in the atmosphere and pedagogy of their instructors and thus that such pedagogy can meet its intended goals. Students' feedback is very valuable in determining whether and in what ways such culturally relevant practices are successful.

In a separate study that incorporated student input, Hughes, Page, and Ford (2011) reported on the perceptions of middle school students: "Rarely, if ever, have the voices of these students regarding culturally responsive practice and cultural dynamics in school been reported in the published literature" (p. 10). Furthermore,

> It is important to obtain the perspective of students attending culturally diverse schools to determine if they perceive that culturally responsive instruction is being practiced and if they believe their classroom and school environments are welcoming and accepting of their culture and traditions. (p. 13)

Participants of the study were 16 "racially, ethnically, and linguistically diverse middle school students with learning disabilities, including low-income, ELL, and immigrant students" (p. 13).

Ranging from fifth to seventh graders at a large urban middle school in the southeastern United States, the participants were enrolled in two special education resource classes (and regular education for other course-work). Understanding student perception of culturally responsive teaching was one goal of the study. Other purposes included learning about student perceptions of their acculturation, their cultural background and traditions, acceptance of their culture at school, and the cultural dynamics of racial and ethnic groups at the school.

Soumah and Hoover (2013) explored students' perceptions of inequality in schools in their qualitative study, in which they interviewed eight high school students. Of the sample, four were African American, three were Hispanic, and one was white. The analysis of students' responses yielded the following themes: academic performance standards and expectations, including curriculum and student motivation; attendance and enrollment issues; bullying and related deportment issues, including consistency of application of discipline and expectations for behavior; equity and fair treatment in school; resources and their effect upon instruction and infrastructure; and diversity and the learning environment.

Students' responses in the area of teacher expectations, decision making, and discipline were the most salient. Students noted inequalities in treatment by teachers and peers, available resources, how discipline was handled at the school, and communication of low expectations. One respondent had very stark perceptions. Yet, the researcher concluded that the student's perceptions did not come from teachers' direct comments because the respondent could not provide that evidence.

Thus, the researcher questioned the construction of the student's perceptions. The female Hispanic student shared that her teachers demonstrated low expectations for her and believed that female Hispanic students would drop out of high school after getting pregnant. While the respondent could not provide direct evidence of her teachers' negative attitudes, the researcher found that direct communication between teachers and students about breaking down negative stereotypes would be beneficial.

In Edwards (2010), two separate questionnaires were administered and the data were used to compare perceptions of teachers and students. The primary intent was to identify whether examples of cultural responsiveness were visible in three separate programs for African American students in a school district with a large population of African American students. One purpose of the study was to determine whether certain tenets of culturally responsive teaching were more important than others. A comparison of responses within and across ethnic and socioeconomic status was made.

The surveys were administered to a sample of 152 African American students in ninth and tenth grade enrolled in three different high schools. Surveys were also sent to a total of thirty-four full-time and part-time teachers. The survey included questions about student perceptions related to cultural identity, self-esteem, curriculum responsiveness, relationships with teachers, program challenge, and cultural diversity. Students gave strong agreement indicators in all areas except student-teacher relationships and self-esteem. They had particularly positive views about working with students from other cultures and learning about diversity (Edwards, 2010).

When students are willing to speak with teachers about their culture, it allows teachers access to students' first-hand accounts of their cultural influences. It can also help teachers avoid using their own cultural frame of reference and pigeonholing students. Instead, they can begin to know students through other frames of reference. Gay (2000) states, "Just as the evocation of their European American, middleclass heritage contributes to the achievement of White students, using the cultures and experiences of Native American, Asian and Pacific Islander Americans, Latino Americans, and African Americans facilitates their school success" (p. 15).

Students should be given opportunities to draw upon their cultural background to make sense of the learning material presented. Gay (2000) sees teachers' cultural responsiveness as a means to increase the achievement of all students but especially for racially, culturally, and economically diverse students who usually demonstrate underachievement. Teachers must tap into who they are and what knowledge and creativity they bring to the learning environment. Their respective cultural heritages and histories that tell the story of who they are must be elicited and affirmed.

Conclusion

The cultural mismatch between teachers and students can no longer be ignored. School administrators and teachers should reflect on how they can meet the needs of such diverse learners. By gathering information about students' perceptions of whether and to what extent their teachers acknowledge, accept, include, and encourage culture in the classroom, teachers and school leaders are able to listen to students' voices. This also shows marginalized students that their perception of and beliefs about their school experience are important and included. Finally, it demonstrates care and advocacy by the school.

Getting to know students on a deeper level than academic indicators like reading and mathematics performance data is crucial. Improving the classroom environment to make diverse students feel welcome and a sense of belonging is required. Furthermore, understanding how students' cultural backgrounds can be springboards for accessing high-quality instruction and thriving in their school experience exemplifies educators' value of all students. Teachers and school leaders must put culturally responsive teaching in place, including considering the student voice.

Eliciting input from students is just as important as knowing students' academic performance information. This chapter focused on the value of student perceptions. The next chapter features an in-depth look at a research study that explored students' perceptions of their teachers in three schools along with insight from the teachers and school principals. The study demonstrates the process of accessing voice and determined whether and to what extent what the students had to say aligned with evidence of culturally responsive teaching.

Student Voices on Culturally Responsive Teaching

A Case Study

Adding to the research on student voice, Fuller (2014) conducted a study with fourth-grade students and their teachers and principals. The perceptions of students, teachers, and school administrators were compiled and analyzed through a qualitative research study conducted in the southeastern United States. Students' perceptions of their teachers and how those perceptions compared to the tenets of culturally responsive teaching were explored. In this chapter, the methodology, findings, and implications of the study are presented.

In addition to the exploration of students' perceptions of culturally responsive teaching, the study revealed teachers' and principals' beliefs about and opinions on the importance of considering race, ethnicity, and culture when instructing students from minority and low socioeconomic groups. It also explored the extent to which students have taken part in or observed cultural responsiveness in their respective classrooms. The study was guided by the following questions:

- How do black and Hispanic fourth-grade students in three Title I–funded elementary schools with predominantly black and Hispanic students perceive their teachers' cultural responsiveness in the learning environment?
- From the perspective of black and Hispanic fourth-grade students, what evidence of cultural responsiveness exists in their learning experience?

- How do the perceptions of black and Hispanic fourth-grade students regarding their teachers compare to the characteristics of culturally responsive teaching?

The study occurred in three elementary schools in one large school district. The schools were chosen because of their large population of black and Hispanic students, the major demographic groups in the schools. Black and Hispanic students were intentionally selected because their voices are often absent from or included minimally in the research that describes them. School demographic information is provided in table 5.1.

Table 5.1. School Demographics

Case	Number of Students	Economically Needy	Limited English Proficiency (LEP)	Black	Hispanic	White
A	830	95%	34%	25%	64%	9%
B and C	1038	92%	33%	15%	74%	8%
D	953	97%	44%	18%	76%	4%

Source: Fuller (2014)

Purposive sampling was used to gather the sample to meet the study's purpose, which was to develop a detailed understanding of the beliefs and perceptions of black and Hispanic upper elementary students. The researcher sought to collect student perceptions, which educational professionals would otherwise know little about. School administrators were invited to select a fourth- or fifth-grade teacher who demonstrated the tenets of cultural responsiveness, had favorable teaching evaluations, and who had been teaching a minimum of three years.

Each case included a very small sample of students and one teacher from four fourth-grade classrooms across three different schools. To allow for in-depth and on-going, one-on-one and focus group interviewing, the study called for between three to five students from each classroom. Interviewing students in upper elementary school as opposed to any other age of students was chosen because limited research on perception of students at this age exists.

While most literature that incorporates student perception is conducted at the high school and college level, some research focuses on middle school (Edwards, 2010; T. C. Howard, 2001; Hughes, Page, & Ford, 2011; Soumah & Hoover 2013). The intent of the researcher was to gain insight into what young learners have to say about their school experiences. After pilot testing the original interview instrument, the researcher decided that upper elementary age students would be able to sufficiently articulate their perceptions through responding to interview questions.

With regard to selecting teacher participants, homogeneous sampling allowed for identification of teachers who principals felt exhibited characteristics of culturally responsive teachers. The teachers also needed to be fourth- or fifth-grade teachers with at least three years of teaching experience and favorable performance evaluations. Based on key points from the literature, specific criteria from which a teacher could be identified as culturally responsive was provided to principals to aid them in selecting the teachers most suitable for the research study. Principals were asked to identify teachers who demonstrated most or all of the following (Brown-Jeffy & Cooper, 2011; Gay, 2010; Gay, 2002; T. C. Howard, 2001; Ladson-Billings, 1995; Toney, 2009; Villegas & Lucas, 2002):

- high expectations for all students
- an awareness that race and culture make up who a person is and influence how life and learning are approached
- respect for diverse races, ethnicities, languages, cultures, background experiences and viewpoints
- orientation to teacher-student relationships and foster parent involvement
- incorporation of multicultural curricula and students' cultural experiences in the teaching and learning process
- a classroom management style that is culturally sensitive
- care for students

Study Participants

Participants provided consent and remained anonymous. Since each school site had at least one teacher participant and four to six student participants, it enabled in-depth probing and data collection given the nature of qualitative study. Table 5.2 lists the demographics of teacher and student participants.

The teacher in Case A was Caucasian and Italian American. A teacher for six years, she had taught at the current school for five years. She attended college in Florida, and her classroom was an exceptional student education cluster classroom. Of the four student participants in Case A, two were Hispanic females whose parents were born in Mexico, one was a Hispanic male whose parents were born in Honduras, and one was a black male whose ancestors were from Haiti and Jamaica.

Table 5.2.   Case Demographics

Case	Teacher Race, Gender	Years of Teaching Experience	Number of Students	Black	Hispanic	Female	Male
A	white, female	6	4	1	3	2	2
B	white, female	11	6	0	6	4	2
C	white, female	22	6	1	5	4	2
D	white, female	5	6	2	3	4	1

Source: Fuller (2014)

In Case B, the teacher was Caucasian from an English and Irish American background with eleven years of teaching experience. A teacher at this school site for four years, she had grown up in a nearby town and followed in the footsteps of her parents and sister to become a teacher. The student sample consisted of four girls and two boys, all of whom were Hispanic. This sample was composed of two Hispanic males with ancestors from Mexico, three Hispanic females with ancestors from Mexico and one Hispanic female whose parents were Puerto Rican and Cuban. Cases B and C were situated at the same school site.

In Case C, the teacher was an Italian American woman from the northeastern United States. Originally a concert musician in New York City, she had lived in Spain and had been in the field of education for twenty-two years. Her husband was Spanish, and she had taught students at the pre-K through university level, including classes of English for speakers of other languages (ESOL). A teacher at the current school for two years, she had taught in other Title–I funded schools in other school districts. The student sample consisted of four girls and two boys. One black female referenced her African American culture. Two Hispanic males were of Mexican descent. One female referenced being half-American and half-Hispanic, and the other two females were born in Cuba.

Case D occurred at the third school site with six student participants and a teacher originally from the northeastern United States. A teacher for five years, this was her first year at the school. She was Caucasian with Italian ancestors and had been raised by a single mother. Student participants included one black and Hispanic female who was of Puerto Rican descent, one black male who was African American and Haitian, one Hispanic female from Cuba, and two Hispanic females from Mexico.

Data Collection

Participants were asked about their experiences with teachers in the learning environment. To begin the data collection process, an interview ranging from 30 to 50 minutes was conducted with each teacher. Interviews were then set up with individual students. These ranged from 7 to 15 minutes. Teachers were interviewed prior to student interviews to relate each teacher's descriptions, examples, and explanations to student responses about their experiences.

Before each interview, the researcher read the children's book titled *What Is Culture?* by Bobbie Kalman. Providing this introduction to the concept of culture prior to the interviews proved to be beneficial in ensuring that fourth-grade students could share their perceptions and experiences with culture. The researcher realized that a definition or depiction of the word "culture" was necessary to ensure that students truly understood the word so they could accurately answer items related to it.

As the study evolved, focus group interviews were conducted in each case. Since students were all in the same class and shared similar characteristics, they could easily draw upon each other's statements and agree or disagree with reliable evidence. Where relevant, teachers' responses from their interviews that occurred first were incorporated in the questions being asked of students during the focus group interviews, which ranged from 25 to 35 minutes. Finally, interviews with principals were conducted. Follow-up focus group interviews with students and interviews with teachers and administrators allowed triangulation of the data.

The indicators of culturally responsive teaching explored included cultural competence; sociopolitical consciousness; high expectations for students; validating cultural differences of students; parent and community involvement; incorporating the cultural background of students in the school experience; utilizing student cultural frames of reference for creating relevant pedagogy; and promoting cultural competence among students (Gay, 2010; Ladson-Billings, 1995; Parhar & Sensoy, 2011; Villegas & Lucas, 2002).

The Voices of Black and Hispanic Fourth-Grade Students

This study was designed to examine the thoughts, opinions, and attitudes that fourth-grade black and Hispanic students exhibited toward their teachers, whom school principals had nominated as culturally responsive teachers, and to further explore teacher practices and beliefs through teacher interviews. This section reports on the results of this study and identifies cross-case themes.

A small sample of students from four fourth-grade classrooms was interviewed at three Title I–funded elementary schools in the southeastern United States. The sample size in each classroom ranged from four to six students. Specific themes included the following:

- having high expectations for students
- parental involvement
- student engagement
- challenge
- cultural awareness
- cultural acceptance
- care

The cross-case themes were having high expectations for students, parental involvement, and cultural awareness.

The interviews also yielded descriptive information, which is presented on a case-by-case basis. Each case includes student responses as well as teachers' responses that relate to the students' particular perceptions. Specific student responses for each case are included in tables 5.3–5.6.

Case A

A theme that emerged from this case was the importance of including parents in their school experience. One student said, "When my parents come in for a conference that means they know really what I'm learning and what the teacher have teached me." The students shared that they and their parents especially like student-led conferences. One student explained, "They're proud to see their kid doing good in school." All students noted a sense of pride about their parents attending the student-led conferences. "I show my mom all my hard work I've been doing," another student stated.

Parents could attend individual conferences with the teacher, contribute to student-led conferences held twice a year in the classroom, participate in phone calls, or write notes back and forth with the teacher. Regardless of the method of parent involvement, participants stated that their parents had communicated with their teacher and felt that such communication was important. Some of these students mentioned their parents' goals for them such as "to be a doctor" or "to pass the FCAT." When asked about the value of parental involvement, the teacher said it was "crucial." She felt that when parents are involved in their student's education, the student feels very proud.

Students were asked about their perceptions of their teacher's expectations. When asked about what their teacher expected them to learn, students noted that the teacher wanted them to do well in their subject areas, be good people, and learn more. Unfortunately, they were not able to identify how they knew their teacher wanted them to do well. One student shared that the teacher said he is "supposed to learn because if we don't learn, we won't have a better life." The teacher responded that the two major attributes her students need are knowing that she believes in them and knowing that she is dedicated to their success as students.

Believing in her students and motivating them to learn and do their best was most important to her. Students referred to their teacher favorably. Yet, their responses were limited in supplying anecdotes in which she had displayed high expectations for them. But the teacher's influence was definitely evident in the following statements: "She always cares for us," "She helps us," and "Whenever we need help, she does the best she can."

It was evident from the data that these students valued the role of the teacher, her positive influence, her high expectations, and the proof of her caring for and believing in them. When exploring students' perceptions of their teachers' cultural responsiveness, it is essential to inquire about their culture and ask how this is included in their learning experience. When asked to describe their respective culture, students were eager to answer and had more to say about this than about any other area of questioning.

Primarily students shared information about their ancestry, religion, foods, special sports, and celebrations that take place with their families. When asked why culture was special to them, the three responses were "You were born with it," "You were born knowing it," and "That's where I'm from so I like it."

Students could not recall a time when their teacher asked them about their cultures specifically. While one student said that the teacher always cared for the students, he was not sure if she knew about his culture. When asked how their teacher incorporates other cultures into the classroom, they stated that the teacher let them draw pictures and talk about their cultures. They shared that she focuses on American culture because she is American. The three students in the focus group interview were sure that their teacher would like to know about their culture and that she would think their culture is important. They said they would be happy to share information about their culture if their teacher asked them.

The final theme in this case was the teacher's acceptance of students' diverse cultures. Despite being "pretty sure she has no idea about our cultures," the students acknowledged that they would like to share their culture with their teacher and felt confident that she would be interested in them. Responding to a question about how she gets to know her students, the teacher explained how students completed surveys at the beginning of the school year and how she took the time to get to know them personally at every opportunity. She did not identify any ways in which she familiarized herself with the particular cultural backgrounds of her students. Likewise, the teacher did not identify how she incorporated the unique cultures of her students into the teaching and learning process. She was confident that the social studies curriculum and textbook served to discuss and incorporate culture. Yet, she did not note any specific examples. She explained that she asks students to write about themselves and share any personal information during writing lessons, and she saw this as a way for students to share their cultural background.

The teacher's responses were confirmed by her students' perceptions. There was no evidence of opportunities for students to share their culture and of including culture in learning opportunities. In fact, students provided ideas about how their teacher could include more cultural activities. These included projects about their culture and other cultures and incorporating students' native or heritage languages in reading and writing lessons.

As one student said, "If she knew about our culture, she could know us better or she should include that in our work. She can know us more." All students agreed that their teacher values culture, and the teacher's responses confirmed that she was aware of how student home environments shape who they are. Thus, the theme derived from this case is cultural acceptance rather than cultural awareness or integration. Student responses in Case A are listed in table 5.3.

Case B

In Case B, the researcher identified the following themes: student engagement, parent involvement, challenge, care, and cultural awareness. These themes are referenced in table 5.4 with specific student responses related to each theme. When asked how they like to learn and which activities are most interesting to them in the classroom, students referred to group work at their tables, discussion with partners, fun writing prompts, listening to music, and being able to talk while doing assignments.

The teacher described several techniques for helping her students achieve: utilizing cooperative learning structures, encouraging student discussion, balancing structure with a free and open environment, forgiving students' mistakes and using them as educational opportunities, providing students with specific praise, giving them rewards when they demonstrate success in the classroom, and incorporating goal-setting.

Table 5.3. Student Voice in Case A

Themes	Participant Responses
Parent Involvement	Parent attends parent conferences and stuac.. conferences
	My parents want me to have a good future.
	I show my mom all my hard work I've been doing.
	She can know how I'm doing in school.
	They're proud to see their kid doing good in school.
	When my parents come in for a conference that means they know really what I'm learning and what the teacher have teached me.
Teacher Expectations	She always cares for us.
	She helps us.
	We're supposed to learn because if we don't learn we won't have a better life.
	Whenever we need help, she does the best she can do.
	Before we do an important test, she reminds us of stuff we learned so we can all get a good grade.
	Trusts.
	Gives respect.
	Betters our future.
Culture	Sometimes [the teacher] lets us draw a picture about our culture.
	If we have to do any assignment about our culture that would be fun.
	I'd be shy to talk about my culture.
	I don't know if my teacher knows about my culture.
	I'm pretty sure she has no idea.
	If she knew about our culture, she could know us better or she should include that in our work. She can know us more.
	If every class has to come up with a culture, like a project about culture, that's a good idea.
	She can give us a little bit of language in our reading and our writing.
	My teacher has not asked me about my culture.
	If I didn't have the same culture and country, I wouldn't be able to communicate with my family in Haiti.
	You were born with it. You were born knowing it.
	That's where I'm from so I like it.

One student explained that they often have instruction on the carpet by the front board, but if the teacher notices that the students are getting bored, restless, or inattentive, then she will give the students a stretch break and change the activity to get them re-engaged. When the teacher provided a

ble 5.4.   Student Voice in Case B

Themes	Participant Responses
Student Engagement	Work together at our table.
	Good to talk with partners
	Helping us when we're stuck.
	When we're sad she says to remember our happy place.
	Reading books that have Spanish words.
	Vocabulary all over the room.
	She asks us to grade ourselves on how we understand it.
	Examples really help.
	Plays music.
	Makes learning fun.
	Doesn't yell.
	If we're getting bored, she lets us take a stretch letting us learn and letting us have fun too.
	When she wants the kids to learn, she doesn't yell or anything but she says time to learn but not in a mean way.
	When she gives us more work, then that's good because we can learn more and you don't have to be talking a lot because you're more interested in the work than talking.
Parent Contacts	When she says good things about you, that makes me feel proud.
	Well, if she's telling my parents that I'm doing really great, then I feel really great.
	Kind of nervous because I might get in trouble.
	I feel like my mom is caring about me so I think it's good for her to know about how I'm doing in school.
	I know meeting with my mom is important.
	I would feel scared if I was in trouble, but just for a student-led conference I wouldn't feel scared.
	Kind of nervous, because I might be in trouble or how I'm doing in school, how's my behavior and how good I am in reading.
Challenge	She gives us bigger words, like when we do our writing,
	She gives us hard stuff on math like so when we grow up, we'll be smart.
	She tells us never give up, try your best and if you still don't get it, we'll check it.
	A lot of work . . . challenges us, entertains us, more practice for the FCAT.
	The teacher should give a lot of work.
	That means she really cares about us and she wants us to do better at our work.
	She challenges us.
	When she gives us more work, then that's good because we can learn more and you don't have to be talking a lot because you're more interested in the work than talking.

Themes	Participant Responses
Care	I think that they should like care about the kids like we care about her.
	She told us everything she tells her son, she does it to us because he goes to school and we go to school and she's a teacher so it's her kid and it's like if we were her kid too.
	She told all of us several times that she cares about us.
	Treat the kids how you want to be treated.
	Gives us a second chance.
	Every morning she says this is a new day and you guys should do your best on everything.
	When we're sad, she tells us to remember our happy place and where we come from and then we all get happy back.
	She tells us never give up, try your best and if you still don't get it, we'll check it.
	When she wants the kids to learn, she doesn't yell or anything but she says time to learn but not in a mean way.
Culture	I'd like to just learn about school stuff like social studies that has different cultures in it but it's telling about something else.
	My teacher already knows about my culture. I think. I'm not sure.
	When we're sad, she tells us to remember our happy place and where we come from and then we all get happy back.
	Some stories we read have my parents' language in it.
	In reading we do have this 4.1 book, and it talks about some of the history throughout the world.

lot of examples and a vocabulary-word wall, students said they felt like they could do their assignments.

When students were asked about whether the teacher had ever spoken to their parents, of the original six students interviewed individually, five said their teacher had met with their parents during a student-led conference or scheduled parent conference. One student stated that the teacher had never spoken to her parents but that her mom did meet the teacher during an open house prior to the start of the school year.

The overall feeling of students was that they wanted their parents to visit the school for conferences and to communicate with their teacher; however, some of the students said that they would be nervous if their parents and teacher met to discuss a problem. When the teacher was asked how the students perceived her contact with their parents, she stated, "If there's ever a conference where the purpose behind it is not positive, I just pull them aside and say I wanna fix this so let's just talk to mom and let's figure it out." She stated twice that she does not like it when the students feel embarrassed so she is sensitive to how they may react in certain situations. The teacher said she encourages all of the students to bring their parents to student-led conferences and tells them, "This is to celebrate you."

If parents were coming in for student-led conferences or to get an update from the teacher on the student's progress in school, then the students reported that they felt happy and proud. They felt their parents cared about them and they agreed that it was important for their parents to speak with their teachers even if it was about a problem. It was evident from student responses that their parents and other family members are so important to them that they want to show them what they are doing in school and how they are progressing. Students also want their families to be proud of their work.

Such student responses made parent involvement a theme in Case B. Students in this case all affirmed that their teacher had high expectations for them. When students were asked how they know their teacher believes in them and believes that they can accomplish their goals, one student stated, "Every morning she says this is a new day and you guys should do your best on everything." Another student knows her teacher has high expectations for her students because the teacher has told them that she has a son and that she treats her students the same way she treats her son.

She requires the students to complete their assigned work and provides incentives to turn in completed work. She does not permit students to turn in a "halfway job." Instead, she provides students with support to follow through with a task and feel successful when they complete it. When asked whether it is necessary to have a teacher with high expectations, the students said yes and shared that teachers show they have high expectations when they provide students with a lot of challenging work.

These students all agreed that they can learn more when they do more work and complete more challenging work. They explained how challenging work would help them pass the FCAT, move through the grades, and have a better life. One of the students shared the idea that a teacher who is too funny and does not provide students with a lot of classwork "probably wants the kids to fail." Other students agreed and said such a teacher would probably have a class that misbehaves by "wasting time" and "goofing around." Students had quite a bit to say about their teacher's caring attitude toward them, which became another theme in Case B.

Students were asked how a teacher who holds high expectations for his or her students would act. Students shared that their teacher treats them the way they want to be treated, encourages them to go to their happy place when they are sad, is always there for them, does not yell at them, gives them second chances, and provides a lot of work. One student gave an example: "She tells us never give up, try your best and if you still don't get it, we'll check it." Another student stated, "She wants the kids to learn. She doesn't yell or anything, but she says it's time to learn but not in a mean way." The students feel motivated to accomplish their tasks because their teacher wants them to do a great job and helps them whenever they need it.

In her interview the teacher explained how she avoided embarrassing students, and they stated that she will talk privately with students when there is a problem. Cultural acceptance was the final theme that emerged for Case B. Students felt their teacher knew about their culture, but they were not sure how she knew. One student faintly remembered telling her teacher about her culture.

All students openly shared their cultural background. They did not recall examples including their culture in the classroom except for citing Spanish words in some reading books and sometimes reading about different cultures. One student stated that she did not want to learn about her own culture. She wanted to learn new things at school and wanted to learn about her culture at home; however, she did recall telling her teacher about her culture. Another student did not understand how the teacher could include her culture and stated that the Mexican culture belonged to her parents, not her. One student mentioned that her religious beliefs prevented her from participating in certain activities and that her teacher would then provide different activities instead.

Although the students could not provide specific examples as to how culture was embedded in their learning experience or how they would like for it to be included, the data showed that students felt confident about culture and felt that the teacher accepted them for who they are. When the researcher asked how she meets the needs of her culturally diverse class, the teacher stated, "You have to realize that they all come from different homes, different experiences, different cultures. I think when you're teaching a lesson first of all you can't make any assumptions and you have to be sensitive to needs." She explained how she respects the religious beliefs of her students by creating alternative assignments to the mainstream Christmas holiday activities.

She described her efforts to remain sensitive to different kinds of homes, experiences, and cultures when planning her lessons and activities. She learns about the students' backgrounds by having parents fill out a form (which asks for any special information they want to provide) at the beginning of the school year. She also referenced activities she uses to understand students' cultural backgrounds and to encourage mutual sharing of these backgrounds. These activities included creating puzzles, completing interest inventories, and playing interactive games.

Case C

The data on student perception in this case helped to identify its themes: student engagement, parent involvement, high expectations, and cultural awareness. Specific student responses related to each theme are listed in table 5.5.

Table 5.5. Student Voice in Case C

Themes	Participant Responses
Student Engagement	When you do something bad, she lets it slide.
	She reviews things.
	She's always doing cheers.
	She gives us high-fives and says, "Great job!"
	We get parties.
	We get a snack.
	With music and mix-pair-share, you can actually move around and not just sit there and do nothing.
	Sharing with partners is kinda fun.
Parent Involvement	It might be great for my parents if they know I'm doing good in classes.
	It's nice if they meet with my parent so that they can tell me what I have to work on.
	My teacher would also know about what I'm doing at my house.
	She needs to let your parents know.
	My teacher tells my parents what's going on and what's getting better and what's getting lower.
	So parents know what to teach more at home.
	She can tell our parents how much we learned and how much we increased in our scores.
High Expectations	She's always like, you can do it, just try it and realize it.
	She pushes us a lot.
	She told me she expects me to have a high reading level.
	She wants us to work hard.
	She's not only working hard with me but she's working hard with everyone in the room.
	She tells us all the time that we're smart.
	I know you can pass this grade.
	She teaches us that she actually cares.
	She knows we work hard to achieve.

Themes	Participant Responses
	I think it's important to have a teacher who has high expectations because when you're not doing what you're supposed to, she reminds you that she has high expectations for you and she makes you feel like you really worked hard.
Cultural Awareness	She's always talking about cultures.
	She accepts what we do from our culture.
	She doesn't talk about my Mexican culture, she talks about cultures from the past.
	She talks about cultures when we're doing social studies.
	Sometimes she speaks Spanish.
	We could all bring in different foods that go with our different cultures.
	She lets us do things that we used to do in our countries.
	Some people don't know my culture and I would like to express it.
	The first day of school she asked me a lot about my culture.
	If she doesn't know us, she doesn't know what we're comfortable with.
	She lets us play the way we played in our country or write the way we wrote in our country.

When asked how they liked to learn, students mentioned sharing their work with others, writing on whiteboards, hearing music, and partner and share activities. The teacher was trained in the Kagan cooperative learning model and was certified to train other teachers. She talked about providing students with ways to learn new information, share their ideas, and solve problems, and she stated that she gives continuous verbal and non-verbal praise to students to keep them motivated.

When asked how their teacher celebrated their successes, the students cited parties, snacks, cheers, high-fives, and compliments like "Great job!" as examples. Students' descriptions of their learning environment illustrated their engagement in what their teacher planned for them. Parent involvement was another theme that emerged. Students mentioned whether their parents had spoken to the teacher and described their thoughts about such communications. One student shared that not only could the teacher share information about his progress with his parents, the teacher would also learn about his home life.

All of the students reported that their parents attended student-led conferences. All agreed that in watching out for the best interests of the student their teacher "needs to let [their] parents know" both the student's positives and negatives. The teacher stated, "If you can get the parents on board, then you've got it all." The students' statements clearly demonstrated their belief that their teacher had high expectations. In the words of the teacher, "I have my high expectations and they know they need to meet them. But I'm also kind and understanding." The students reported that their teacher repeatedly said they are smart, they could pass the grade, and she expected improvement in their test scores, reading levels, and grades. They also mentioned that she was always pushing them to learn more and perform to their best ability. The final theme in this case is cultural awareness.

The researcher asked students to share details about their respective culture, describe how their culture was included in their classroom, and discuss how they would like their culture to be included. The students freely shared information about their culture, including languages their family members spoke, the countries their parents or extended family had come from, special traditions and celebrations, and important beliefs. Similarly, the teacher shared a lot about her cultural background in the interview. She had lived and taught in Spain, Honduras, and Japan and was married to a Spanish man. She talked about her family's struggles when returning to the United States and her husband's difficulties adjusting to a new culture.

When answering the researcher's questions, she often related her answers to her own cultural background and professional experiences. One student said it best: "If she doesn't know us, she knows what we're comfortable with." When explaining how culture is incorporated in the classroom, the students mentioned that their teacher sometimes spoke Spanish to them, talked about cultures during social studies instruction, and let students express different cultural backgrounds through academics as well as socially. For example, one student who was born and educated in Cuba said that she is glad her teacher allows her to incorporate Cuban phrases in her writing because she can express herself more easily.

Case D

The data in the final case yielded the following themes: building relationships with students, high expectations of students, parental involvement, and cultural awareness. Specific quotes within each theme are found in table 5.6. The students perceived that their teacher took the time to build relationships with them. They believed that she knew what they liked and were interested in. One student described how the teacher placed a little note of encouragement on her desk, while another mentioned a classroom prize box filled with items the students could request.

Table 5.6.   Student Voice in Case D

Themes	Participant Responses
Building Relationships with Students	If you had a big even coming up, it's super exciting, she'll not go home, she'll stay here and she'll go to that event and see you either perform or whatever it is.
	We have a prize box.
	We get treats.
	She buys us Justin Bieber and One Direction.
	She helps us to do it step by step.
	She's a real fun teacher.
	We get to do a bunch of projects, instead of just sitting there and looking around.
	Make us more confident.
	When we didn't try our best the one day, she writes a little note and puts it on our
	desk the next day and writes you can do better, you know you can.
Parent Involvement	She sends this certificate home and the parents be so glad and we get to hang them up.
	I want my parents to know how I'm doing in school.
	I think it's important for them to talk because if something's going on in school and it's really bad they need know about my grades and so they can like talk to me about it and they could also help me to learn about it.
	My parents really want me to succeed in school.
	My parents would know stuff that I don't even know.
High Expectations	She's always telling us to learn many languages because the better we are with languages, the more jobs we're going to get in life.
	She knows that we can pass it because even if we are a little lower, she's pushing us and pushing us.
	She's gonna start to pushing us and pushing us til we reach our goal.
	She always says we can do our best.
	She challenges us with things that may be a little harder.
	She says you can do it.
	She says this goes for everybody in the classroom.

The teacher shared the importance of tracking student successes academically to keep them motivated to put forth their best effort. The teacher confirmed that she would write the students personal notes as well as give them some of their favorite things as rewards. She mentioned "making a connection outside of the academic" to help motivate them. The students and the teacher felt that special events outside the school day were important for helping them get to know each other. The teacher believed the students need "somebody who shows an interest in their lives outside of school."

Holding high expectations for students was another theme identified in the research. Students confirmed these expectations when they described how the teacher pushed them to work hard and achieve. Providing them with challenges was a way of holding them to high expectations. One student observed that her teacher would not have given them a writing word wall and other learning activities if she did not have high expectations for them. One student's perception was that her teacher's goal was for her to do "very good in school and life and have a good career."

The focus group students also agreed that the teacher's preparations for state exams showed her high expectations. She tells them that they can reach their goals. Students also perceived parental involvement as very important. One student joyously reported that the teacher sometimes sends home certificates of accomplishment and that her parents are very happy with her when she receives one. Another student stated that her parents' goal is for her to succeed in school. The teacher confirmed her students' perception of the value of parental involvement, describing this as "probably the most important thing."

Of the three students who took part in the focus group interview, one student's parent attended a conference, one's aunt came to a conference, and one student's parents worked a schedule that did not permit them to attend any school conferences. They all agreed that they wanted their parents to know how things were going for them in school.

The final theme of this case is the perception of the teacher's cultural awareness. When the class read a story that included information about a different culture, the students reported that the teacher would identify the country's location on a map and ask if any students had something to share about that particular culture. One student recalled a time when the teacher pointed to Haiti on the map and asked about Haitian culture. This reminded the student of her Haitian father.

Although the students could not provide rich descriptions in their statements, the students in the focus group shared that the teacher accepts and acknowledges diverse cultures and wants them to "come together just like a family." They noted that she compares and contrasts cultures and that she lets all the students express special information about their cultures.

Listening Across Cases: Common Themes

This section explores the perceptions heard across cases through the voices of students and summarizes the themes that emerged from all three cases. Students' perceptions of their teachers' cultural responsiveness emerged in different ways. Likewise, each teacher said different things about their students and offered different perspectives about what they needed for success. While this study did not yield generalizable findings, the researcher found several cross-case themes: holding high expectations for all students, parental involvement, and cultural awareness.

To varying degrees, all students referenced their teacher's high expectations and faith that they could achieve at the same level as peers in the school and district. The students valued parental involvement even though some students were nervous or scared if they were in trouble. Finally, the data collection yielded significant dialogue about student culture and student attitudes toward using culture to help them learn. Even though the degree to which students elaborated on cultural factors varied, the students all recognized their teachers' cultural acceptance and awareness in the classroom.

High Expectations

The teachers consistently maintained that holding students to high expectations was imperative, and this was confirmed by the students' perceptions. Across cases, students believed their teachers had high expectations because they assigned challenging work and pushed students to reach their goals. When asked whether the teacher had the same expectations for all students and thought that all students could do their best, the students always said yes. They felt their teacher demonstrated these beliefs by expressing clear expectations, explaining how to meet those expectations, and helping them to do so.

Students also demonstrated their perception of their teacher's high expectations by stating their teacher knew their preferred learning styles, believed in them, and celebrated their successes in the classroom. The following themes from within cases are part of the larger theme or support the larger theme of holding high expectations for all students: building relationships, care, student engagement, and celebrating success.

Parental Involvement

Not all of the students interviewed had parents who attended teacher conferences, but they all agreed that it was important for parents to be involved in their school experience. Those students whose parents had not had contact with the teacher stated that they would like such contact. Students' perceptions of parent-teacher communication were mixed because many viewed parent conferences as punitive and negative in nature.

However, even students who saw conferences that way acknowledged that the teacher and the parent should talk about the child's strengths and weaknesses so parents were informed. The students expressed fear and nervousness if they were unsure of what information the teacher would share or if they were "getting in trouble." Their perception of student-led conferences, however, was much more positive; students demonstrated pride and happiness that their parents had an opportunity to learn about their school experience.

Valuing Culture

Students did not hesitate to provide information about their personal cultural background. They were happy to share what they knew about their unique background and experiences, and they displayed a sense of pride and engagement. They also shared insights about how they view and value culture related to their learning experience. Teachers' and students' thoughts aligned on the importance of valuing and embracing the personal background and home lives of students.

Across all cases, students perceived that their teachers were interested in and accepted their culture although some students were not sure if their teachers actually knew about their culture. Overall, the descriptions of how teachers included culture in the classroom were limited. Student perceptions varied. Some did not perceive any particular cultural awareness being included while others described classroom discussions about culture when related to reading curriculum. The students also supplied ideas on how to include more culture in the school.

Reactions of School Administrators

At the conclusion of the data collection and analysis, school administrators' initial reactions to the findings in each case were sought. Each school site's principal or another administrative designee was invited to participate in an interview. Principals in cases A and D agreed to participate. No reply was made by the third principal—the school administrator in cases B and C—after several attempts. The administrator was asked to comment on each theme with an immediate reaction to the findings. The interview concluded with a question related to the administrator's thoughts on the value of the student voice.

The interview with the principal in Case A took place at the school site and lasted approximately thirty minutes. The administrator agreed that each of the themes—building relationships, high expectations, parent involvement, and cultural awareness—was crucial to the success of students. He shared that building relationships is crucial and that teacher and student must work together to build that relationship, whether it is writing notes to the students, rewarding them for their efforts, or simply talking to the students. The principal added that this teacher, in particular, attended a ballet performance put on by the students at a nearby high school, which highlighted her efforts in attending school-community events.

Regarding the teacher's high expectation for her students, the principal acknowledged that teachers should not let student deficits in certain academic areas hold the students back from having rewarding classroom experiences. He referenced this teacher's use of technology, higher-level questioning and thinking techniques, multiple opportunities for sharing, and meaningful and engaging lessons in which students of all ability levels could feel validated. The principal affirmed the teacher's response that parent involvement was crucial.

He emphasized the personal aspect involved with getting to know parents during extracurricular or community events at the school. He referenced taking the time to speak with parents whenever possible and building partnerships despite language barriers. One student, the teacher, and the principal all referenced a National Honor Society program in which the teacher stayed late to support her students and take the time to get to know their parents and families.

A final reaction by the principal was in the area of the teacher's cultural awareness. He referenced the importance of culture within the classroom so that all students' backgrounds and identities were supported and celebrated just like a family. He noticed that it is very clear in this classroom that all students are respected and accepted. When asked about the value he sees in work on student perception and listening to the voices of students, he stated that it is very powerful and that the "student voice is really the most important voice."

The interview with the principal in Case D took place at the school site and lasted approximately twenty-five minutes. The principal was eager to hear the researcher's findings. The major themes were parent involvement, high expectations, and cultural acceptance. With regard to parent involvement, the principal agreed that it is vital and noted that it is important for teachers to not only rely on scheduled student-led conferences but to also reach out to build relationships with parents at other times. She wants teachers to go above and beyond to make these connections with parents.

In the area of high expectations for students, the principal agreed that holding students to high standards allows them to work toward reaching goals and helps them strive for success. The principal mentioned the importance of providing focused feedback and praise so that students are aware of how they can reach these expectations. She stated that teachers should really be "highlighting their achievements and accomplishments" and that this "promotes ownership in them wanting to do better."

Regarding the final theme of cultural acceptance in this case, the principal shared that students love any chance they get to share who they are—their cultural identity, their classwork, and their interests—and that this should be welcomed. Although the teacher did not identify specific ways to pull in students' cultural background and frames of reference, the principal agreed that this teacher welcomed students' diversity but did not see evidence of how their backgrounds were incorporated.

The principal wanted each teacher to see the uniqueness that makes up every child and said that if the teacher included that in the learning environment then school would be more relevant to students and they would have more success. Noting the value of research on student perception, she stated that surveying students is just as important if not more important than surveying staff. She stated, "They're our customers, and they are who we are here to serve." In closing, she noted that student achievement is of utmost importance, and students are one of the keys to it.

Conclusion

This chapter presented black and Hispanic fourth-grade students' perceptions of their teachers' cultural responsiveness. The researcher interviewed a small sample of students in four teachers' classrooms. After analysis of the data, the themes across the four cases were identified as holding high expectations, parental involvement, and valuing culture. Prior to the emergence of these cross-case themes, the researcher carefully reviewed the coding to find themes within each case. Other themes specific to particular cases included care, challenge, cultural awareness, and cultural acceptance.

The study's goal was to tap into the voices of upper elementary–age black and Hispanic students as they expressed their perceptions of their teachers' culturally responsive practices, an area of research that is limited within the latest literature on culturally responsive practices in schools. Since school systems serve students from a diverse range of socioeconomic statuses, ethnic origins, and cultural norms, teachers must be equipped to teach within a culturally responsive framework and not just the cultural code they are accustomed to (Gay, 2002; Shealey & Callins, 2007).

The increasing cultural mismatch between white teachers and a diverse student body creates a challenge for schools seeking to eliminate the racial achievement gap. Thus it can be very valuable to learn what students think about how teachers create positive learning environments, present culturally relevant pedagogy, and help students connect their cultural background with their learning experiences (Gay, 2002; T. C. Howard, 2001, 2003; G. Howard, 2006; Ladson-Billings, 1995).

~

CHAPTER SIX

The Teacher's Cultural Autobiography

A Tale of Perception, Belief, and Bias

As much as teachers must get to know their students to teach them effectively, teachers must first learn about themselves and their development with respect to their own culture and underlying perceptions, beliefs, and biases about teaching diverse students. Teachers and school leaders should identify whether they know enough about their own respective culture and what has shaped their current frame of reference for decision making in the classroom. Furthermore, they should consider how self-analysis and a cultural autobiography could be a step toward best supporting their culturally diverse students.

What teachers believe about their students becomes their expectations for those students. Teachers may hold students to lesser expectations without even realizing this. Bias affects how beliefs, opinions, and perceptions materialize in teacher actions in the classroom. How teachers interpret student behavior through their own cultural lens determines for the teacher how they relate to students. In interactions with students, we teachers "bring the baggage of our past experiences, our prejudices, and our preferences" (Davis, 2012, p. 12). This chapter explains the cultural autobiography process and its importance in reducing bias toward diverse students.

Meaningful reflection should take place while a teacher is identifying his or her philosophy of education during teacher preparation; however, anyone who has not yet participated in this introspection should begin immediately. When a teacher hasn't learned about and had experiences with diverse students, assumptions may run wild. Teachers who operate on assumptions show a lack of understanding of high expectations, parental involvement, and other characteristics of culturally responsive teaching.

A teacher's bias interferes with children reaching their full potential both academically and with regard to social and emotional development. Bias may appear in the classroom as low expectations of minority students, failure to elicit parent involvement because of the assumption of poor minority parent involvement, not using differentiated lesson planning based on unique student needs, and not acknowledging or valuing differences. Students are forced to accept this as the "way it is at my school," and the hope for inclusivity and overcoming cultural mismatch is then shattered.

Teachers' negative beliefs and perceptions often perpetuate the underachievement of minority groups. Ladson-Billings (2007) identifies the most common teacher perceptions of minority and low SES students as parental apathy, limited student experience, lack of preparation to begin school, and poor living conditions. While any number of factors may influence a student's education, guessing which ones do or assuming that all minority students are affected by these factors is unacceptable.

Building positive relationships with students and conducting parent conferences with all parents to understand the child's background is a crucial role of teachers. Becoming informed leads to positive outcomes while choosing to align with assumptions perpetuates marginalization of minority students. The teacher is either an advocate for overcoming cultural mismatch or chooses to ignore his or her role in discovering positive outcomes for all students. Some examples of the bias of teachers and administrators include the following:

- having lower expectations of bilingual students
- having lower expectations of students with immigrant parents
- believing that students in single-parent homes will always struggle
- believing that black and brown people are all disadvantaged
- believing that minority parents do not care and do not help their children
- believing that all minority students are poor
- believing that black students spend more time on sports than homework
- believing that minority students are not gifted and talented
- believing that minority students do not intend to go to college

Teachers must overcome these misconceptions before they can truly engage with culturally responsive pedagogy. Understanding that all school personnel hold their respective beliefs about educating minorities and beginning with the creation of a cultural autobiography are ways to initiate the thoughtful introspection required to identify bias as well as process how it may affect teaching and learning in the classroom (Hammond, 2015).

The cultural autobiography is a powerful process for self-examination of personal bias. In their study of a preservice English teaching program in which they studied the use of written cultural autobiographies, Gunn et. al (2013) state, "Written reflection can serve as a tool to gain individuals' knowledge of self and others, and through their own self-awareness individuals recognize connections to and differentness from others" (p. 2).

Teacher Perceptions and Beliefs

This section examines the literature on the ideas and opinions of teachers regarding culturally responsive practices. Literature in the area of teacher perceptions and beliefs is somewhat limited. Most studies focus on teachers of African American students and concentrate on the problem of the black–white achievement gap; however, a few major studies have influenced the field, including Edwards, 2010; Ladson-Billings, 1995, 2009; Toney, 2009; and Walker, 2011.

Toney (2009) conducted a qualitative study that investigated how the backgrounds and experiences of teachers affect their teaching of African American students. Specifically, the study focused on how teachers' respective cultures influenced their teaching. Toney's representative sample included four sixth-grade teachers from a suburban middle school near a major midwestern city. The teachers participated in interviews, observations, and focus groups.

Additionally, researchers sought to understand how teachers' beliefs and perceptions compared to what was actually observed in the classroom. The study's data analysis described how the teacher could develop instruction focusing on students and that drew from their cultures, hold up high standards for all students, and make use of the teacher's experiences and personal reflections (Toney, 2009).

Examining the black–white achievement gap, Walker (2011) analyzed teachers' perceptions of African American students. The intent of the researcher was to analyze the data for evidence of deficit thinking. The three areas of focus were perceptions of teachers, cultural competence of teachers, and teacher effectiveness as it related to their perceptions of their students' cultures. For this qualitative study of ten elementary school teachers in a large urban school district, the study's criteria for participants included teaching mostly African American students and having at least five years teaching experience.

The study used purposive sampling as a way to allow for rich, contextual data. Teachers were selected through principal nomination, and data was collected through the conduction of two semi-structured interviews. Walker (2011) identified a common theme among the recorded perceptions of teachers: "The teachers attempted to put forth an ongoing effort to understand the students' cultural backgrounds at various levels and used that knowledge to assist in facilitating successful outcomes" (p. 583).

In another study, Parhar and Sensoy (2011) looked at the cultural responsiveness of ten teachers in a Canadian school district. Although the researchers were not specifically seeking teachers of African American students, participants were nominated based on their effective use of culturally relevant pedagogy. The nominated teachers were required to self-report that they employed at least five of the tenets of culturally responsive teaching to be considered for selection in the study. Five elementary and five secondary teachers were selected.

The study sought to discover how teachers who are committed to providing culturally responsive learning environments describe their beliefs, perceptions, and challenges in carrying out their commitment. Researchers found that teachers who understand and follow culturally responsive practices are guided by its principles to advance the academic and social achievement of "culturally minoritized students" (Parhar & Sensoy, 2011, p. 192).

The authors further explored the importance of culturally responsive teaching as they expressed the most valuable tenets of the instructional implications. Connecting students' prior learning from their native language and values is one practice that culturally responsive teachers employ regularly in classroom instruction. Parhar and Sensoy (2011) list additional attributes of cultural responsiveness in schools:

- teaching curriculum from multiple perspectives
- learning about students' unique cultures and learning styles to make learning more meaningful
- creating and maintaining high expectations and standards for all students
- creating engaging, challenging, motivating, and cooperative lessons
- working to mold a community of learners in the classroom to emphasize an inclusive setting
- validating the personal identities of students in terms of culture

- encouraging a caring and respectful learning environment that invites students to think critically about academics, social issues, and discriminatory structures
- building relationships with students that are built on mutual respect

The research of Ladson-Billings (2009, 1995) was designed to report highly effective teachers of African American students and to disprove common perceptions about the continual low achievement of African American students. This qualitative study examined the perspectives, teaching, and reflections of eight teachers over a two-year period in northern California. These teachers were determined to be teachers of excellence by both parents' and principals' standards. Of the teachers, five were African American, three were white, and all were female. They had been teaching for twelve to forty years, mostly with African American students. Their reflections on what was important in teaching African American students was based on daily teaching experiences. During ethnographic teacher interviews, they shared their range of knowledge, background, and experiences. The teachers were not limited to a particular script but were asked to expand on any topic they thought had value. These areas included family background and education, perspectives on teaching, pedagogical theory, and social issues. Data were also collected via classroom observations, notes, videotape recordings, and reflective comments and clarifications provided by the teachers.

A research collaborative conducted by the teachers was a particularly powerful portion of the study in which the teachers examined their practices and those of their colleagues. This research collaborative allowed teachers to "re-examine and rethink their practices" (Ladson-Billings, 1995, p. 473) and share their teaching approaches with each other. Regarding the communication and dialogue as pertinent to the process of acquiring knowledge, Ladson-Billings states, "Rather than the voice of one authority, meaning is made as a product of dialogue between and among individuals" (p. 473).

Popp, Grant, and Stronge (2011) conducted a study with a similar intent to Ladson-Billings in which they sought to explore the characteristics of highly effective teachers of at-risk students. Teacher behaviors were studied through classroom observations, and interviews with each teacher were conducted to note their perceptions of and beliefs about teaching. From the perceptions of the teachers emerged the following findings: affective and academic were intertwined; assessment was integral to meeting student needs; meeting basic needs of students was needed; high expectations had to be maintained; and success had to be measured.

The Case for a Cultural Autobiography

A cultural autobiography is a reflective, self-analytic story of an individual's past and present. Narváez et al. (2013) state, "Autobiographies depict with words life stories, personal experiences, and perceptions" that enable others to realize the "way people see life, reflect, and construct meaning out of experiences" (p. 1). In a framework created by Hammond (2015), awareness is one of four crucial components for effectively teaching culturally diverse students. Within the awareness phase, the teacher is encouraged to "know and own your cultural lens." Hammond states,

> I define culturally responsive teaching simply as an educator's ability to recognize students' cultural displays of learning and meaning making and respond positively and constructively with teaching moves that use cultural knowledge as a scaffold to connect what the student knows to new concepts and content in order to promote information processing. All the while, the educator understands the importance of being in a relationship and having a social-emotional connection to the student to create a safe space for learning. (p. 15)

Along with Hammond's desire to prepare teachers to become "emotionally conscious culturally responsive educators," "acknowledging diversity as a positive element of the classroom is vital and by reflecting on the challenges that can interfere with open acceptance of students who are different from you in background, race, class, language, and gender" (p. 53).

Adding to the value of the cultural autobiography process to guide teachers toward cultural responsiveness, Narváez et al. (2013) state, "Autobiographies as a way of narrative have become paramount in the teacher education field and, indeed, have become a lens to explore and facilitate understanding of teaching practices and to delve into the what, the how, and the why of pedagogical actions" (p. 2). Hammond (2015) states, "Even educators who have taken an explicit social justice or progressive stance have implicit bias based on their exposure to the dominant culture's messages and memes over a lifetime" (p. 29).

To expose problems that marginalize minority students such as implicit bias and racism, identifying these tendencies is the first action teachers must take. Understanding whether they hold negative beliefs and opinions about minority students and how those may hold students back from reaching their potential is another layer of introspection. Directions for teachers to complete the cultural autobiography process, including specific questions, are included in appendix A. The questions include but are not limited to topics of racial and ethnic identity, nationality, childhood, adulthood, and experiences with people of other backgrounds. Implicit bias and structural racialization in schools are what Hammond (2015) describes as the "bookends of the sociopolitical context," which hold a system of inequality in place (p. 29). Operating involuntarily, implicit bias "refers to the unconscious attitudes and stereotypes that shape our responses to certain groups" whereas structural racialization is "deeply connected to the relationship between where one lives and how location and geography affect one's access to education and job opportunities, as well as other quality-of-life factors" (p. 29).

A few examples of structural racialization include placing less-experienced teachers with no proven performance in classrooms with the neediest students; masking the literacy challenges students face rather than providing resources aligned with weaknesses to specifically address areas of weakness; and focusing more on accountability related to state testing than creating plans of action to help struggling students make real progress (Hammond, 2015).

Students, teachers, and school leaders must collectively work to expose racism and overcome its divisiveness. How and why teachers choose what to do in their classrooms should not be based on each teacher's interests or convenience but should be determined based on student needs stemming from their cultural backgrounds. Teachers should understand how and why they feel or react a certain way regarding interactions with students.

Preservice teachers must have knowledge and skills in this area as well so that they can be active facilitators of change as new teachers, thus breaking the cycle of masking these inequalities. Preservice teachers who then become first-year teachers in diverse school settings with overwhelming cultural mismatch will be better equipped to utilize students' cultural backgrounds when planning and delivering instruction.

Hammond (2015) aims to bridge the divide of cultural mismatch and includes four practice areas for teachers that can be taken on as self-study but may be better suited for professional development or study groups. While awareness, learning partnerships, information processing, and community building are designed to work in unison, Hammond states, "Learning to put culturally responsive teaching into operation is like learning to rub your head and pat your stomach at the same time. . . . The trick is to get each movement going independently then synchronizing them together" (p. 18).

Taking preservice teachers through a process in which they create their own cultural autobiography through answering key questions, sharing their responses in conversations with others, and engaging in critical dialogue they likely never have had before on topics that affect students of ethnic, cultural, and socioeconomic diversity is crucial because "if teachers do not know how their own cultural blinders can obstruct educational opportunities for students of color, they cannot locate feasible places, direction and strategies for changing them" (Hammond, 2015, p. 18).

Teachers must be "aware of the impact of their own cultural lens on interpreting and evaluating students' individual or collective behavior that might lead to low expectations or undervaluing the knowledge and skills they bring to school" (Hammond, 2015, p. 18). Underrepresented students continue to be marginalized. Teachers are called to serve as front-line advocates for students, ensuring high expectations and value for diverse backgrounds.

This action helps teachers "locate and acknowledge their own sociopolitical position, sharpen and tune their cultural lens, and learn to manage their own social-emotional response to student diversity" (Hammond, 2015, p. 18). Thus, a teacher can begin to realize through this process how his or her beliefs about groups of students could be the driving force behind choosing how to interact with them, discipline them, and teach them. Select sample reflections of preservice teachers are included in appendixes B through F.

While Hammond (2015) explains that many elements of culturally responsive teaching must work together, culturally responsive teaching cannot begin until teachers tap into the vital component of awareness. Without taking the time to look inward and examine bias through perceptions and beliefs, teachers are not getting to the core of the issue: overcoming cultural mismatch through getting to know students and self. All teachers must invest time in intentional introspection and writing a cultural autobiography, thus reflecting upon the current beliefs and assumptions that have become their unique cultural lens.

Gay (2018) suggests that the knowledge and skills teachers need regarding the pedagogy should be "complemented with careful self-analyses of what teachers believe about the relationship among culture, ethnicity, and intellectual ability; the expectations they hold for students from different ethnic groups; and how their beliefs and expectations are manifested in instructional behaviors" (p. 81). Choosing instructional techniques and management and discipline techniques complementary to students' cultural backgrounds affords students of diversity equitable school experiences.

In addition to the latest trends for addressing the achievement gap, Hammond (2015) calls for teachers to be self-reflective and to consider changing themselves "especially when our students are dependent learners who are not able to access their full academic potential on their own" (p. 52). Reflection by the teacher is needed to be fully aware of students' needs and to respond in culturally responsive ways.

Inclusive Discussions on Race, Culture, and Teacher Bias

In addition to creating a cultural autobiography, it is imperative to invest in opportunities to share it and learn from others' personal stories. The dialogue that follows is just as important as the creation of the product. Individuals who have never created a cultural autobiography need practice in sharing their viewpoints and values in this sensitive area. Additionally, what is important to them may not be nearly as important to someone else or not important at all.

One of the most crucial phases of the cultural autobiography process is initiating discussions among participants about their individual written reflections. Whether preservice teachers or veteran teachers or administrators who have never undertaken the process are engaging in dialogue, these conversations bring together beliefs and values and help participants realize how they shape their view of the world, decision making, and ultimately teaching.

Just as when an individual creates a cultural autobiography and becomes engulfed in his or her personal story, wanting to tell it but also reflecting on what it means or how it has shaped them, so does someone else who is eager to share theirs. Everyone has a story. Everyone has a voice. Prior to reading about and participating in this process, individuals may not have taken the time to really think about who they are and how that shapes them and drives their decision making, teaching, disciplining, and so forth.

A positive climate for discourse on race, culture, and teacher bias must be created to maintain an environment of respect and inclusivity. In matriarchal African American culture, the grandmother's home is a place of safety, acceptance, care, and belonging. It is an environment where many people feel welcome to share stories, recall memories, and listen to the voices of family, friends, and acquaintances. This type of engaging environment where voices are heard, differences are present but not dividing, and everyone walks away respected should be fostered to initiate discussion on the process of the cultural autobiography.

Some of the reflections and realizations stated by participants may be of a sensitive nature. Participants should be reassured that they only need to share what they are comfortable with including. They can also bring to light areas of bias that they desire more knowledge about. The presentation of the cultural autobiography includes an explanation by the presenter but may also include questions being asked by others. This is another layer in the process that naturally produces an experience in which participants can listen to and consider the experiences of others. A climate of mutual respect is crucial for this exercise. The following are some ways to generate this discourse, creating meaningful opportunities to learn from and about others.

- *Entire staff professional development:* Staff members complete their cultural autobiography individually using a narrative, digital presentation, or other format; share with a small group of two to four people during staff development time; create a plan of action for next steps
- *New teacher training opportunities:* New teachers are provided professional development in the area of cultural responsiveness and overcoming cultural mismatch; new teachers are trained on how to complete their cultural autobiography individually and then create a narrative, digital presentation, or other format; new teachers and teacher mentors share their experiences, or the group of new teachers comes back for a discussion and to create a plan of action for next steps.
- *New teacher and mentor opportunities:* Staff members complete their cultural autobiography individually using a narrative, digital presentation, or other format; new teachers and teacher mentors share their experiences as pairs and then with another pair of mentors and mentees and create a plan of action for the next steps
- *Faculty focus group:* Select staff members who are interested in showing leadership in completing the process, being trained, and being able to bring the information back to their team of teachers attend training on overcoming cultural mismatch and creating a cultural autobiography then create and share a cultural autobiography within the focus group.
- *District-wide focus group:* Select staff members who are interested in showing leadership in completing the process, being trained, and being able to bring the information back to their school of teachers attend training on overcoming cultural mismatch and creating a cultural autobiography then create and share a cultural autobiography within the focus group.
- *Professional development training in addition to actual teacher contract:* This would serve as optional professional development training that would be available to staff during after-contract hours. Members would attend the training, complete a cultural autobiography, and come back and share the experience.
- *Part of a preservice teacher-education university course:* The creation of the cultural autobiography is a wonderful experience for preservice teachers who may be enrolled in a cultural diversity course or any similar course (e.g., cultural awareness, multicultural education, etc.). At smaller colleges and universities that may not have these courses, the process could be conducted within a classroom management course. The creation of the cultural autobiography should take place after lectures and

readings. Students in pairs or groups of three should share their products with each other and rotate peers to share with multiple individuals.

- *Part of preservice teacher-education internship seminar:* The process of creating a cultural autobiography would also be a good fit for students enrolled in a diverse teaching internship as supplementary work to engage in and reflect on their readiness to work with diverse school students. It will also allow these preservice teachers to begin the journey of culturally responsive teaching.

Conclusion

Cultural mismatch, the racial achievement gap, and social and emotional development challenges must be addressed and solved in U.S. public schools. One way to do this is for teachers to take part in the self-analysis and written reflection embedded in the process of creating their own cultural autobiography. Research on teachers' perceptions of culturally responsive teaching shows teachers' active roles in improving outcomes for minority students. Teachers must realize that individuals' unique experiences make up who they are, how they make decisions, how they interact socially, and how they learn.

These experiences comprise the respective cultural lenses through which we perceive the world around us. These cultural characteristics make up a person's total being and who they are. Through answering probing questions such as those in appendix A, teachers can begin to determine their bias and how that may play a role in how they approach teaching and classroom management. These ideas will arise from focused conversations on how marginalized students may feel about school and the role teachers play in that.

Within schools, teachers and school leaders may embark upon this great feat by participating in the creation of a personal cultural autobiography. Taking an introspective look and identifying bias and how that affects instructional decision making and disciplining of students is a step in the right direction. All students have diverse backgrounds, upbringings, beliefs, and opinions that make them who they are. Knowing exactly who students are and how their backgrounds have shaped them is of utmost importance.

Teachers should identify the demographic composition of the students in their classrooms and then complete a self-assessment to determine what is known about their students' cultures and what similarities and differences are shared. Learning about the cultures of students is important and can be done through interviewing the student and parents or family members, studying different cultures at local colleges or universities, engaging in diverse community events, volunteering, and more. Individuals may experience a feeling of being "out of their comfort zone," which provides a learning opportunity to develop empathy and awareness for underrepresented students.

Finally, teachers and educational leaders are encouraged to complete their own cultural autobiography. A cultural autobiography is a personal story of a person's cultural background. Through considering a list of both superficial and deep prompts, individuals can begin to reflect on how their own personal background has shaped their current cultural lens. This includes considering nationality, racial/ethnic identity, views on religion, gender, opinions of the pre-K through twelfth-grade educational experience, influence of parents, and social status.

Deeper questioning may elicit personal beliefs and biases that provide individuals with an opportunity to accept or correct their perceptions. Breaking down assumptions and stereotypes, school personnel must confront their misconceptions and biases and identify gaps in knowledge and understanding. To be considered are perceptions related to how respect is taught and demonstrated; parental involvement in teaching morals; family values and the importance of doing well in school; experience with individuals who differ in cultural and ethnic backgrounds; and bias toward certain groups of people as well as discovering the source of that bias.

Through dialogue, individuals can share their cultural lens and some of the understandings and misconceptions that were identified through the process. Completion of a cultural autobiography alone is not enough to springboard school personnel into becoming culturally responsive; therefore, of greatest importance is the discourse centered on an individual's cultural lens and how it informs planning and decision making in teaching, classroom management, and discipline.

CHAPTER SEVEN

~

A Perfect Picture
of Cultural Mismatch

A Case Study

Cultural mismatch is on the rise in the United States with rising numbers in minority student enrollment. Carver-Thomas (2018) states, "A quarter of first-year teachers in 2015 were non-white, up from 10 percent in the late 1980s. However, the teacher workforce still does not reflect the growing diversity of the nation, where people of color represent about 40 percent of the population and 50 percent of students" (p. v). Realizing that people are most familiar with where they grew up, the local demographics, and the diversity, or lack thereof, school professionals must be aware of national demographics and how they are changing.

The State of Florida has the third-highest enrollment of public school children in the United States. There are 2,832,424 students in grades pre-K through twelfth grade, behind California with 6,304,266 and Texas with 5,401,341 (Florida Department of Education, 2020). Of the full-time instructional staff in the State of Florida, 70 percent, or 143,451 individuals, are classroom teachers. The 2019–2020 school year racial and ethnic demographics of Florida teachers are listed in table 7.1.

Cultural mismatch in Florida's schools can be extracted from the data in table 7.2, which is the percentage of teachers and students by race. Minority students in Florida's schools will likely encounter cultural mismatch or already are encountering it due to the fact that the percentage of minority teachers is smaller than that of minority students. While specific school demographic information will vary, 67 percent of Florida's teachers are white while only approximately 37 percent of the state's students are white. Approximately 63 percent of Florida's student population identifies as a minority or non-white.

Table 7.1. Florida Teacher Racial/Ethnic Composition Data

	Asian	Black/African American	White	Hispanic	Two or More Races	American Indian/ Alaska Native	Native Hawaiian/Other Pacific Islander	Totals
Elementary Classroom Teachers	1%	12.5%	67.9%	17.2%	1%	<1%	<1%	74,447
Secondary Classroom Teachers	2%	15.4%	66%	15.3%	1%	<1%	<1%	69,004
Totals	1%	13.8%	67%	16.3%	1%	<1%	<1%	143,451

Source: Florida Department of Education (2020)

Table 7.2. Demographics of Florida's Teachers and Students

Race/Ethnicity	Number of Teachers	Number of Students
Asian	1%	2.8%
Black/African American	13.8%	21.6%
White	67%	36.7%
Hispanic	16.3%	34.7%
Two or More Races	1%	3.7%
American Indian/Alaska Native	<1%	0.3%
Native Hawaiian/Other Pacific Islander	<1%	0.2%

Source: Florida Department of Education (2020)

Exploring Cultural Mismatch in the Southeastern United States

In the study discussed below, preservice teachers of the southeastern United States were asked to share their beliefs and perceptions related to preparing to teach in a diverse school setting. The purpose of the study was to explore the perceptions preservice teachers had about creating a cultural autobiography during undergraduate teacher-education courses as well as their perceptions of teaching diverse students. Another purpose of the study was to then compare how these perceptions related to the tenets of culturally responsive teaching.

The study was guided by the following central questions:

- From the perspective of preservice teachers, what are their respective experiences with creating a cultural autobiography for the first time?
- How do preservice teachers at a private, religious university perceive teaching black, Hispanic, or low SES students?
- How do preservice teachers' perceptions of their experiences when creating a cultural autobiography compare to the characteristics of culturally responsive teaching?

The study revealed preservice teachers' beliefs and opinions about the process of creating a cultural autobiography as a useful springboard to beginning culturally responsive practices. It also identified their perception of the importance of considering race, ethnicity, and culture when instructing students from minority and low SES groups. Preservice teachers in the university's teacher preparation program participated in field observations and internships in the local public schools. In this chapter, the design and results of the case study are discussed.

The racial and ethnic composition of the student population where the study took place has been increasingly diverse. From 2011 to 2020, the number of Hispanic students increased from 47 to 52 percent and the number of white students decreased from 37 to 33 percent. Black students make up 11 percent of the student population, with the remaining 4 percent of students identifying with other races. More than 61 percent of the students are considered economically needy. In 2020, 16 percent of students were classified as learning English as a second language.

Currently 7,500 students in K–12 are enrolled in the English Language Program, an increase of 1,000 students from 2011. Collectively, the students speak 104 different heritage languages and hail from seventy-six different countries of origin. Fifty-five percent of students live in non-English homes where English is not the first language and sometimes is not spoken at all, which is an increase from 46 percent in 2011.

This study occurred with preservice teachers from a private, religious university. The participants gain preservice teaching experience with diverse students at local public schools for a total of four semesters of practicum and internship. Most of these schools have a majority of black and Hispanic students living in poverty. Study participants were identified based on their enrollment in a university course in which they created a cultural autobiography as a course assignment.

Grounded in social cognitive theory and sociocultural perspective, the study sought to gather and analyze preservice teachers' self-reflections on their experience of writing their cultural autobiography and perceptions of teaching diverse students. Kim and Baylor (2006) state, "Social-cognitive theories emphasize that teaching and learning are highly social activities and that interactions with teachers, peers, and instructional materials influence the cognitive and affective development of learners" (p. 1).

Pajares (2002) states, "Social cognitive theory is rooted in a view of human agency in which individuals are agents proactively engaged in their own development and can make things happen by their actions" (p. 1). Narváez et al. (2013) state,

> The sociocultural perspective is a fairly new one which entails the theoretical ground to explain and conceptualize teacher learning, language teaching and teacher education overall. In this line, this perspective sustains the value of autobiographical accounts in the examination of what is behind student-teachers' beliefs and how their practices are or may be the reflection of their previous experiences as social individuals. A fundamental principle of a sociocultural theoretical perspective is that human cognition is understood as originating from and fundamentally shaped by engagement in social activity. (p. 2)

The cultural autobiography assignment involved students reflecting on and responding to a number of questions. These questions were both surface level and deeper in nature. The personal introspection led participants to write a self-reflection on their culture and begin to investigate how their own lens of culture informs how they view, interpret, and react to the world around them. This self-analysis encourages participants to consider their childhood through adulthood. Then participants are encouraged to analyze their cultural lens related to teaching diverse students in the public school setting.

Participants created a presentation with pictures, symbols, and talking points that they then shared in pairs. The process included students sharing their product several times with different peers, rotating through several partners. This allowed for conversation instead of simply presentation, and students gained practice and confidence sharing their personal beliefs, values, and opinions. Directions for the assignment, including questions students used to get started with their reflections, is included in appendix A.

To begin the data collection process, an electronic questionnaire was sent to eighteen students. Eight returned the initial electronic questionnaire. Of those participants, seven were seniors, one was a junior, five were education majors, three were minoring in education, and seven planned to become full-time teachers. Three participants in the initial survey were invited to participate in the second round of questions. They are referred to as participants A, B, and C to protect their identities. All three were white, female, senior education majors. Descriptive information about each of the three participants can be found in table 7.3.

The second electronic questionnaire was conducted with the three selected preservice teachers and it included additional and more specific questions to elicit deeper thoughts and opinions. As themes emerged from the responses to the original questionnaire, the researcher developed these additional questions to investigate certain avenues of inquiry to deepen understanding and allow for a wealth of description. Statements made by participants that were interesting, vague, or enlightening were taken into account when designing additional questions to encourage elaboration.

Preservice Teachers' Perceptions
of the Cultural Autobiography Process

These findings add to the work of others in the field. Preservice teachers' perceptions of creating a cultural autobiography is a limited body of research. Taking the time to look inward, reflect, and create a cultural autobiography

Table 7.3. Preservice Teacher Participation Description

Participants	Preservice Experience with Diverse Students	Self-disclosed Ethnic/Cultural Background
Participant A	Semester freshman year of urban teaching cohort; tutor and soccer coach in impoverished area in southeastern United States; preservice teaching experiences in Title 1 schools with majority of diverse students	I am white and from a Chicago, Illinois, suburb. I am mostly Italian and Lithuanian. This has shaped me as I have grown up in a European household that has shaped a lot of my tendencies and actions. I also grew up in the middle class, which has largely shaped my outlook on life.
Participant B	Preservice teaching experiences in Title 1 schools with majority of diverse students	I have much experience with diverse backgrounds as my parents were foster parents and cared for kids of all backgrounds. My experience has showed me that every person is unique and should be valued. A person's background and experiences help us learn more about that person and helps us value them for who they are.
Participant C	Preservice teaching experiences in Title 1 schools with majority of diverse students; virtual English teacher for Chinese students	Caucasian/American. I grew up in the Midwest where I lived in a suburban neighborhood. I went to predominately white schools throughout my life and then was exposed to more cultural diversity upon attending college in southwest Florida. I traveled abroad to Rome my sophomore year, which changed my life. My sense of culture was immensely broadened, and now I have dreams of traveling abroad extensively.

is crucial for preservice teachers. Awareness includes learning how others perceive the world around them and ultimately take in information, communicate, and learn (Hammond, 2015).

The focus of the study was to explore participants' respective experiences when creating a cultural autobiography for the first time. The study additionally explored how they perceived teaching black, Hispanic, and low

SES students and how their perceptions of creating a cultural autobiography compared to the characteristics of culturally responsive teaching. In this section, the resulting themes will be shared as well as a discussion on how the results relate to culturally responsive teaching.

Preservice teachers favorably viewed the process of creating a cultural autobiography (analyzing how they respectively view the world and discovering their own cultural lens; Hammond, 2015). On the first electronic questionnaire, 37.5 percent of participants strongly agreed that after creating the cultural autobiography they felt equipped to teach diverse (non-white) students whereas only 12.5 percent strongly agreed prior to the experience.

More specific, detailed, and thematic results were gleaned from the specific, open-ended questioning of the second questionnaire. Regarding preservice teachers' perceptions of the process of creating a cultural autobiography, the data analysis produced the following themes: meaning, need, and relevance. More specifically, participants found meaning and value in the process; saw the necessity for the experience and the growth opportunity it provided; and recognized a connection with what was important, which is educating students of diversity.

Meaning in the Process

The purpose of taking preservice teachers through the cultural autobiography process was to illuminate the need for aspiring teachers to undertake self-analysis. All of the participants in the initial questionnaire administration agreed that completing the cultural autobiography process was meaningful to them as future educators. Participant B stated, "A person's background and experiences help us learn more about that person and helps us value them for who they are."

Preservice teachers' time and effort spent on the cultural autobiography enabled them to think about their beliefs and opinions and how those were constructed over time and were of great importance and value to them. Taking this time is an intentional step in teacher preparation. Answering personal reflection questions, sharing their autobiography with peers, and engaging in discussion were valued by all of the participants.

Participants took genuine interest in listening to their peers' stories about their life experiences. Out of these paired conversations came validation, celebration, understanding, and curiosity. Listeners could ask clarifying questions in seeking to understand others' unique stories. Preservice teachers valued their experiences in creating the cultural autobiography as part of their undergraduate coursework in their teacher-education program. Participant responses on the meaningfulness of the process are contained in table 7.4.

Table 7.4.   Perceptions of Preservice Teachers

	Perceptions of Preservice Teachers			
	In What Way(s) Was Creating a Cultural Autobiography Meaningful Process to You?	*What Did You Learn from This Process?*	*What Did You Learn That Helped You Support Diverse (Nonwhite) Students?*	*How Did the Process Prepare You For Your Current Teaching Position?*
Preservice Teacher A	I got to see how my experience was and reflected upon it and how it may have affected my schooling. It was mostly beneficial however because I got to see people's reactions to my past and I got to see what others experienced in their pasts.	I realized more that people's past shaped their world views and their entire mindset in life.	I learned that I need to provide my students with a holistic experience approach and provide background knowledge for everything. I realized that a lot of assumptions I make are only geared to my own personal views and I should not make any generalizations or assumptions about students' childhoods.	It mainly provided insight on to how I responded to my schooling experience as a child. From there I realized what I needed to do differently in order to not teach according to my own personal needs but for all needs of all students. It also brought in to my horizon what is normal for students of different cultures.
Preservice Teacher B	I liked the cultural autobiography project because I learned much about my friends that I did not know about their lives even though we were close friends. It helped me to make deeper connections and relate to them in a better way.	It is important for my students to have good, and meaningful relationships. I think it is most important that all my students feel respected and valued for who they are.	No response recorded.	No response recorded.
Preservice Teacher C	It was incredibly relevant for me, as a teacher in where none of my students share my exact culture. It helped me to practice cultural awareness and begin to develop a greater sensitivity.	I learned that everybody sees the world from a different lens and the cultural autobiography helps our peers to see a better glimpse through our lens, and vice versa.	I learned that just because what might be considered normal for me and my family, doesn't mean it is normal for my students and their families.	It helped me to be prepared for the differences I would encounter. I can remember my first week I experienced A LOT of shock. First with my two boys who spoke only Spanish; that was a challenge of language barriers.

The Need for Planned Self-Analysis

When asked in the initial questionnaire if they agreed that learning about the diversity of their students was necessary, all participants agreed. Participants thought it was necessary to partake in the process during their preparation to not only teach diverse students but to specifically teach students with very different ethnic and cultural backgrounds from them. It was seen as an opportunity for growth and required some to step out of their comfort zone.

Chartock (2010) states, "For teachers preparing to implement culturally responsive teaching, one of the most useful first steps is to explore your own cultural influences and connections" (p. 27). One participant went on to share that the process prepared her for working with diverse students by "providing me with other people's experiences and mainly showing me what my main tendencies and beliefs were." Another explained it was necessary for "help[ing] me to think deeper in understanding that we all have been given different sets of values from both sides of our parents/guardians, which has helped form our own unique values."

Participant C stated that when she started her teaching career she felt ready "to encounter the different values, traditions, and customs that come along with those individual mindsets." The process aids preservice teachers in moving in the right direction toward learning about others, affirming differences, and including diversity in positive ways in the classroom. The activity brought about awareness by helping students pinpoint their own cultural lens and experience listening to and learning about that of others.

Making It Relevant: Connection to Teaching and Beginning Culturally Responsive Teaching

A third theme touched on the importance of the cultural autobiography. In addition to being meaningful and necessary, the process was relevant to the participants. They expressed positive connections between the self-analysis within the cultural autobiography process and the desire to work toward meeting the unique needs of diverse students. All of the participants in the initial questionnaire recommended this process to their peers; 87.5 percent enjoyed sharing their cultural autobiographies with peers; and 87.5 percent said the process helped them learn about themselves.

Participants found the overall activity to be applicable to their coursework as aspiring teachers. The self-analysis, written reflection, and purposeful discourse on findings were all related to their current studies. Preservice teachers become knowledgeable in evidence-based practices for literacy instruction, differentiation, cross-curricular connections, classroom management, cooperative learning, formative assessment, and more. In this same way, how to reach and teach diverse students through culturally responsive teaching, beginning with teacher reflection, is significant to overall effectiveness of the beginning teacher. It is relevant to the development of the preservice teacher and must be included in teacher preparation programs.

Cultural Autobiography and Characteristics of Culturally Responsive Teaching

Key to gathering beliefs and perceptions is making sense of the responses. In this section, participants' perceptions are summarized within the context of the following tenets of culturally responsive teaching: high expectations for all students, cultural competence, teacher–student relationships, and designing curriculum and instruction.

High Expectations for All Students

The preservice teachers in this study were aware that students of diversity and students in poverty must have a teacher who holds them to high academic standards and helps them find success in school. Holding all students to high expectations is one key tenet of culturally responsive teaching. This finding emerged as participants cited the importance of high expectations for students and the importance of forming relationships with the students. Relationships were described as key to understanding students' background knowledge and skills and supporting them by scaffolding their learning when necessary.

Through relationship-building, high expectations can be communicated to students. Examples of the expectations that participants held for their students included students doing their best, being charitable to others, trying to learn, and being able to achieve the same as others. The teachers saw students as successful based on their work, test scores, the smiles on their faces, interest in learning, effort, and active engagement.

One participant stated, "I can see that they care about meeting their goals." Preservice teachers must take part in diverse teaching experiences to be prepared to teach all students to high levels. It is important to note that 87.5 percent of participants in the initial questionnaire agreed or strongly agreed that the process helped develop understanding and empathy for others.

Participants also shed light on their perception of parental involvement. Chartock (2010) states, "Students of all backgrounds and income levels are more likely to have success in school when classroom community building involves strong parent-teacher communication and partnership" (p. 47). Keeping parents abreast of important information and incorporating parent

Table 7.5. Preservice Teachers' Perceptions of Parent Involvement

	What Value Do You See in Parent Involvement?	How Should Teachers Interact With and Include Parents and Families?	How Do You Include Parents/Families and Their Cultural Backgrounds?
Participant A	I see lots of value in parent involvement. My students who have highly involved parents are constantly striving to do better and impress people outside of me myself. When the parents do not care the child does not care either. It is a very big issue in my classroom.	Teachers should interact with and include parents and families through constant interaction. Teachers should have a platform where they can share student progress with parents.	I allow for students to share about their past and bring in articles that pertain to their family and give them projects that ask their family's history.
Participant B	I think parent involvement is crucial. Parents need to know that their involvement in their child's education can play a major part in their success. Parents need to feel that they can help their child. Parents also need to know that they are valued for who they are. Parents need to be included and know what is happening in their child's class.	No response recorded.	No response recorded.
Participant C	I see value in what educational extensions are happening at home. Parent involvement shows the students that other people care and are invested in their learning so they should be too.	Teachers should keep parents in the loop with their child's achievements and classroom behavior. It doesn't need to be daily of course, or even weekly, but there needs to be some form of communication.	I include them by keeping in touch via Class Dojo, and just recently I joined the parent involvement leadership as a part of our schools 7 Habits platform.

input and involvement in the teaching and learning process is essential. Participant responses are included in table 7.5.

Cultural Competence

Cultural competence refers to "manifesting your personal values and behaviors and the school's policies and practices in a manner that is inclusive of cultures that are new or different from yours and the school's" (Lindsey et al., 2009, p. 17). Gay (2018) states, "Cultivating the competence and confidence needed to implement culturally responsive teaching should begin in preservice teacher-education programs and continue in in-service professional development" (p. 287). Practice must complement knowledge.

Based on participant responses, it cannot be said that they had achieved cultural competence. Results show that participants agreed that the backgrounds of diverse students were important and that the cultural autobiography process was valued. The results do not suggest that participants attained cultural competence; however, preservice teachers did experience some development with cultural awareness and sensitivity.

Participants responded to questions about how they plan for what culturally diverse students need and shared examples of engaging lessons. Additionally, they spoke to how they come to know what students need, how they incorporate students' backgrounds, how they establish and maintain a culturally sensitive classroom, and how they account for cultural diversity. Responses, however, did not provide sufficient depth to confirm cultural competence. Further questioning either individually or in focus groups to probe evidence of cultural competence is recommended.

According to Villegas and Lucas (2002), a socioculturally conscious teacher "recognizes that there are multiple ways of perceiving reality and that these ways are influenced by one's location in the social order" (p. 21). One purpose of this study was to examine whether the process of writing a cultural autobiography for preservice teachers could serve as a springboard to the overarching goal of culturally responsive teaching. In the initial questionnaire, 100 percent of participants agreed that ensuring all students learn, no matter their racial or ethnic background, is crucial.

While participants did not state actions for addressing the racial achievement gap of continued underperformance of black and Hispanic students compared to white students, the self-analysis undertaken by the participants and their willingness to reflect upon it in this study shows that participants cared about inequities they learned about and experienced during their teacher education and practice. Completing the cultural autobiography process within their teacher preparation program introduced them to the shift in thinking required and the self-analysis involved in being a reflective practitioner.

Teacher–Student Relationships

The relationship between the teacher and student is the foundation for communication and action in the classroom. It is a vital component of the teacher's ability to provide high-quality teaching that takes into account students' unique cultural backgrounds. The teacher–student relationship was valued by the study participants. Participants viewed differences as strengths. Moore (2007) notes that care and concern are among the defining factors of a culturally responsive classroom environment.

Celebrating success and avoiding deficit thinking (Ladson-Billings, 2007) support strong teacher–student relationships. Participant C stated, "Students feel excited and express joy upon their successes" while Participant A stated, "When students feel successful they are more confident in the attempt to achieve even more." Positive affirmation, verbal praise, tangible rewards, and recognition were examples of celebration given. Participant C stated, "I am very conscious about verbal praise and telling [students] I'm proud of them for their effort."

Participants were asked to identify what they saw as the key attributes that students need in their teachers. The participants shared that students need someone they can trust and talk to and someone who cares about them. Participants shared that the key attributes students need in them as their teacher are care, trust, and being a listener. Participant C stated that she needed "to be someone who listens and responds to them in a way that values [student] dignity."

Designing Curriculum and Instruction

Results from the initial questionnaire showed that all participants agreed that incorporating students' backgrounds and cultures in the teaching and learning process is important. Participant A stated, "Students can learn most when they can connect with the information personally and it applies to their direct situation." Other responses in the area of curriculum and instruction included visuals, hands-on tasks, scaffolding, one-on-one instruction, and explicit instruction applying directly to students' needs. Parhar and Sensoy (2011) ascertain that student cultural frames of reference should be incorporated in the child's instruction.

Frames of reference are how a child views his or her environment and takes in information (Gay, 2010), and the educational process should feature and integrate each child's cultural background (T. C. Howard, 2001;

Villegas & Lucas, 2002). Preferred learning styles are part of the child's lens and should be taken into account during teacher planning (Gay, 2000). When asked how they come to know what students need, participants cited student-work reviews, conversations with students, individual "check-ins" with students, a suggestion box, monitoring student engagement, and creating joy in the classroom.

Participants were asked to more specifically detail how they plan for the needs of culturally diverse students. Asking students to share their own personal experiences was listed as one of the ways to support students. Other responses included scaffolding material, mentioning different cultures, considering what kind of things culturally diverse students will relate to, and calling upon instructional support personnel at the school for resources and support. Specific responses are included in table 7.6.

The Cultural Autobiography
as a Springboard to Culturally Responsive Teaching

This study's participants valued the process of creating a cultural autobiography and believed the process as well as their experiences with diverse individuals and students all contributed to their development as beginning teachers. The process of creating a cultural autobiography allowed the students to look inward. They answered questions that were both surface level and very deep. They had an opportunity to share about themselves, learn about others, and converse with peers on issues related to race, ethnicity, and all of the aspects of a person's background.

Preservice teachers must be prepared in university programs to reach and teach all students in the nation's schools. This includes teaching students of diverse backgrounds that will likely differ from their own. As a result, cultural mismatch exists. Teachers must be willing and ready to work with students from all backgrounds, forming relationships with them and partnering with their parents. Diversity must be viewed as an asset and not as a deficit or a hindrance to learning and development.

Beginning the process of culturally responsive teaching should occur during undergraduate work. Preservice teachers learn that introspection is needed as well as deep reflection on how an individual's beliefs and perceptions inform how one approaches key decisions in education. Some of these topics include managing and organizing the classroom, building relationships with students and parents, disciplining students, identifying and addressing language barriers, addressing special education needs, understanding the effects of poverty, and planning to teach a wide variety of content.

Table 7.6. Incorporating Students' Culture in Their Educational Process

	In What Ways Do You Incorporate the Cultural Backgrounds and Experiences of Your Students?	In Terms of Classroom Management, Are There Ways You Are Culturally Sensitive?	When Choosing Curriculum Planning Lessons, How Do You Account for Cultural Diversity?
Participant A	I incorporate the backgrounds and experiences of my students by allowing for lots of opportunities to share personal stories and personal connections. They are always allowed to write about their work and mention their experiences.	I am culturally sensitive in particular to the African students in my class for example they are used to lots of movement and constantly moving therefore they struggle to sit still. I provide them learning goal leader positions in which they can move and stand very often. I also allow for flexible seating. Students are allowed to move and sit wherever they are most productive as long as they are being productive and complete their work.	When choosing curriculum and planning lessons I decide on activities that will allow students to share their personal experiences and experiences that will allow them to use their preferred learning methods.
Participant B	I let my students express their different home and life experiences with their peers. I provide them with many opportunities to communicate and work together. For example, one student read a book to the class in Spanish.	No response recorded.	No response recorded.
Participant C	I like to use social studies time to have discussions about where we come from and share with each other. I also make sure to use read-alouds about other cultures.	Yes! I make sure I allow more leeway with my Haitian boys because I know their bodies usually need to be moving. I will let them stand and do their work.	I think about what they will need additional explaining of—for example if it is something very rue for American culture only, they will need some background knowledge. I make sure to be very explicit with vocabulary words, showing a visual and giving examples.

Introspection is key to understanding self and beginning to hear, realize, and understand others and how they interpret the world. The professional disposition of "room for growth," or considering whether it is important to make space in your heart and head for considering if and how teaching diverse students may be unintentionally affected by your own beliefs and values, should be developed as early as possible in the preservice teacher's education or teacher's career.

Thinking about and answering challenging questions that may not have been previously considered is crucial for deep reflection, personal growth, and development toward acknowledging and understanding personal difference and the natural bias or beliefs attached to difference of race and ethnicity. All teachers should reflect upon their thinking to become the best facilitator of knowledge for their students.

All preservice teachers in teacher-education programs should have access to coursework that includes self-analysis related to their background. They also need to be immersed in meaningful conversations with others about their cultural autobiography, with opportunities to learn and discuss how this experience helps them prepare for teaching in diverse schools. Reflecting on working in a diverse setting and completing an autobiography allow for continued discussion and further reflection. It is never too late for a preservice teacher or even veteran teacher or administrator to write their cultural autobiography for the first time.

Conclusion

Undergraduate teacher preparation programs must incorporate creation of a cultural autobiography in the curriculum. Solely completing a course requirement of compiling information on self is unacceptable; a protocol for introspection and discussion should be incorporated in depth (Hammond, 2015). Opportunities for reflection on student teaching experiences through journaling and discussion are also essential. All preservice teachers should be exposed to teaching in diverse school settings. It is counted as a disservice to preservice teachers when this is not afforded to them.

Developing awareness and beginning these conversations is only the tip of the iceberg. Taking preservice teachers through this self-reflective process to identify feelings about diversity is not enough to affect achievement without continuing personal and professional development and accompanying this awareness with culturally responsive pedagogy in action (Gay, 2015). Gay states, "Positive recognition of and attitudes toward ethnic and cultural diversity are necessary but not sufficient for dealing effectively with the educational needs and potentialities of ethnically diverse students" (p. 287).

If preservice teachers do not have an opportunity to take this essential look inward, discovering beliefs and perceptions, they are unprepared to begin teaching in their own classroom upon graduation from a teacher preparation program. This gap in knowledge will result in the preservice teacher being unprepared to teach all students. "All students" means all students. When we fail to consider bias toward and misconceptions held about diverse students, a fundamental component required in being able to reach and teach those students has been overlooked.

CHAPTER EIGHT

~

Implications for Practice

Practical solutions for schools to address cultural mismatch are given in this chapter. Several mechanisms will be highlighted. These include a framework for overcoming cultural mismatch, an inclusive schools action plan, college and university teacher preparation program considerations, and recommendations for further research. Through employing targeted, research-based practices, critical issues facing students can be proactively and collaboratively addressed. Solutions are sought with voices from students and parents in addition to school personnel.

A Framework for Overcoming Cultural Mismatch: Roles of Teachers and Administrators

The goal of this framework is to activate the teacher–student relationship and the student–school experience in a way that values student voice—student perceptions of their experience in school, the influence of their culture, and how they believe school professionals can utilize these insights as a springboard for effective teaching and learning (see figure 8.1). The voices of the students provide valuable information about themselves and valuable information for teachers and school leaders to consider regarding the classroom environment and instruction.

The framework is a guide for teachers and school leaders to help position themselves to actively engage underrepresented students and incorporate their cultural backgrounds. Davis (2012) states, "The school culture deter-

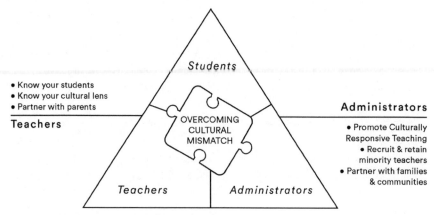

Figure 8.1. Framework for Overcoming Cultural Mismatch: Roles of Teachers and Administrators.
Source: Laura K. Onuska

mines, in part, the academic achievement of its students. Our perceptions (our cultural lens) determine, in part, the academic achievement of our students" (p. 98). Steps and ideas for creating a plan of action for shifting to culturally responsive teaching practices are discussed, and priorities for teacher preparation programs are detailed. Finally, some recommended areas for future research are given.

The framework also serves as a tool for overcoming cultural mismatch and helping the teacher move in the right direction toward a shift in thinking about the valued role of a student's cultural background in the classroom. Further, it moves teachers closer to being able to begin culturally responsive teaching, which includes broad ideals and can be overwhelming to implement. Using the framework as a guide, teachers and administrators can commit to equity in their schools today with an actual foundation on which to do so.

Culturally responsive teaching is not a set of steps or a checklist to follow. Preservice and newer teachers may not have the requisite skills to successfully embark upon this shift in thinking and teaching. Teachers and school leaders should use the framework as a readiness tool to begin to engage in culturally responsive teaching. Even experienced teachers may have a difficult time initiating this shift.

These concepts illustrate a practical approach for teachers and school leaders to begin to do their part to promote equity in classrooms and schools. The framework identifies roles for both school leaders and teachers. Support for teachers is imperative as they work to enact their action steps. These steps encourage school personnel to consider a philosophic shift in thinking toward working to narrow the racial achievement gap in schools.

Several mechanisms are in place for teachers to begin to overcome the negative effects of cultural mismatch in their classroom. These include the teacher getting to know his or her students' cultural backgrounds, getting to know his or her own cultural background and level of cultural competence, and building partnerships with parents and families. School leaders must be culturally proficient and promote culturally responsive teaching practices. In addition, they must recruit and retain minority teachers and partner with parents, families, and community organizations. The steps provide school personnel with realistic starting points for moving in the right direction toward quality educational opportunities for all students regardless of race, ethnicity, or cultural background.

The mechanisms are in no particular order of importance; however, teachers must actively engage in all three to be ready to learn about and implement the tenets of culturally responsive teaching. Thus, teachers must actively get to know students, take part in self-analysis, and build parent and family partnerships as soon as possible in the school year.

For school administrators, the framework offers a high-level look at school culture and planning for professional development, taking into account retaining a diverse teaching staff and partnering with parents and community organizations. Administrators should consider all points prior to beginning the school year. Another consideration is how overcoming cultural mismatch will help meet the school's overall school improvement goals. Eliciting partnerships with the community extends beyond businesses to nonprofit organizations and places of religious worship that share a vested interest in social justice.

The Role of the Teacher in Overcoming Cultural Mismatch in School

Get to Know Your Students

As teachers prepare instruction for their students each school year, they consult students' respective data from previous years. In this way, an academic, statistical picture of the student is formed; however, teachers can no longer use solely this quantitative information to prepare for planning how to best meet the needs of their students. Teachers must consider the qualitative data that is generated when they get to know students on a personal level like cultural factors, social and emotional characteristics, and special interests. Asking students about themselves is the best way to understand them and avoid making assumptions.

Cultural influences, when considered, can only enhance the learning environment, strengthening engagement, motivation, and achievement. Teachers can learn about students' cultural identities through inventories, interviews, small group discussions, and even by students themselves writing a cultural autobiography. When the teacher takes the time to learn about students' cultures, it shows that he or she acknowledges culture. It also shows they value the background of students and the role it plays in student learning and achievement.

Understanding that students' specific beliefs, perceptions, actions, and behaviors all begin with their cultural lens allows the teacher to develop empathy for differences. This leads to listening, patience, asking the student for his or her point of view, and promoting solutions over division. Building a relationship with student requires the teacher to not just "walk in the shoes" of the student. The teacher should envision "spending a day in the life" of the student. The teacher must truly ask him- or herself, "What would I do if I were in the same situation?" It is important to know and consider the cultural lens of the student.

Get to Know Yourself

The perfect time for practicing teachers to write their cultural autobiography is prior to the beginning of the school year. If the school year has already begun, it is not too late. Plan to use in-service days while engaging in meaningful discourse centered on reflections made on race, ethnicity and bias and their implications for education.

The process includes reflecting on many questions (see appendix A). Some questions are simple, and others are more thought-provoking. There is no time limit for this endeavor and several weeks or more would be ideal so that individuals have ample time to ponder most of the questions. Some questions may lead participants to consult immediate and extended family members. Not all of the questions need to be answered. Questions can be skipped or partly answered if individuals have sensitive areas upon which reflection is difficult.

The amount of time dedicated to the process varies as some individuals are very aware of their cultural influences and others are not. How the individual compiles his or her responses also affects the overall time for the task. Writing a narrative, writing a speech, or creating a digital presentation with photos are some of the ways individuals may choose to prepare their product. Finally, dedicate time to share these personal reflections with others in pairs or very small groups. This is the culminating activity.

If the process is undertaken by schools, parameters for these steps should be established by the school leader or designee. This individual should facilitate the dialogue portion by keeping time for sharing, encouraging teachers to share with more than one individual or small group, and finally by guiding deeper discussion once all participants have had an opportunity to share their story. Steps can be adjusted as needed to fit the needs of the participants; however, do not eliminate the sharing and discussion as this is when the deepest connections are made.

Preservice teachers should complete a cultural autobiography in their teacher-education program. This must be paired with instruction on the tenets of culturally responsive teaching while maintaining an overall philosophy of education. Embedding this in field observation or teaching experience is ideal.

Parent and Family Partnerships

Parent and family partnerships should be established and fostered at the beginning of the school year. They should be maintained through weekly or monthly newsletters, parent conferences, parent nights, student-led conferences, and so on. Some of the best ways to begin genuine partnerships with parents and families include being welcoming by offering a warm greeting, shaking hands, making eye contact, smiling, and displaying positive body language. Being friendly and making personal connections with parents demonstrates value for the parent and gives the impression that the teacher and school are on their side.

The goal in building parent partnerships is to discover the expectations the parents have for their child. Next, partner with the parents to interweave classroom expectations with what the parents expect. This enables parents to feel like equal partners in their child's success. Teachers have an opportunity to share with parents classroom strategies that support students in meeting high expectations. These include social and emotional skill-building, goal-setting, utilizing formative assessment, modeling higher-order thinking, use of mentors, teaching test-wiseness, promoting the value of reading, and teaching communication skills.

The Role of the School Administrator

Promote Culturally Responsive Teaching

For the school administrator to implement, model, and teach the practices of culturally responsive teaching, he or she must be culturally competent.

School-level and district-level administrators must demonstrate cultural competence and take part in activities to strengthen this area. Acquiring culturally competent school administrators must be a priority for districts. Administrators must ensure they have the knowledge to lead the way with culturally responsive teaching.

Practicing teachers who have not received training in culturally responsive teaching practices in their college or university teacher preparation program may have never heard of this pedagogy for reaching and teaching diverse students. Likewise, even teachers who may recall some undergraduate coursework in this area likely do not know how to begin even though they may philosophically align with the theory. Still more, teachers who have been alternatively certified and did not participate in a traditional teacher preparation program will likely not demonstrate readiness for culturally responsive teaching.

Recruit and Retain Minority Teachers

District- and school-level administrators must determine if their recruitment and retention efforts are sufficient. Likewise, district and school administrators must promote a culture of inclusion for both students and staff. This includes maintaining a culture that implements culturally responsive teaching and culturally responsive practices within the school. This works to ensure individuals of color feel a sense of belonging in the workplace.

For many students of color, the school experience is not a positive one that incorporates their cultural background or even relates to them. Encouraging these individuals to return to school as teachers is nearly impossible. Once the nation's schools become more responsive to and inclusive of diversity, slowly there will be a shift toward more minority candidates enrolling in teacher preparation programs. This will take time. As more and more teachers commit to all students, more positive experiences and favorable outcomes for students will result.

Build Family and Community Partnerships

School administrators must be aware of the importance in many cultures of working collectively. They must create school environments that are welcoming places that allow parents of diversity to easily access activities, parent-teacher conferences, resources, support, and the like. The school culture must be one that exudes inclusivity for all. Inviting parents to volunteer and be a part of the school day, establishing a parent resource center, and offering English language classes and parenting classes are some possibilities for creating and sustaining relationships with parents (Davis, 2012).

In addition to the partnerships that must be founded with parents, schools have a unique opportunity to partner with community organizations and members that can offer support and services leading to student achievement. This should not be limited to business partners but should include local churches, community groups, and nonprofit organizations whose mission support causes related to social justice and equality. Schools can invite community members to talk about diversity and race relations and offer training for parents in crucial skills like computers or finances.

Administrators must work to build a culture of empathy, seeking to discover the experiences of others without making assumptions and perpetuating stereotypes. Administrators must take the time necessary to meet with parents of students with academic and disciplinary red flags. Planning to support at-risk students in a proactive manner will aid in setting the student up for success. Create opportunities to meet and greet parents before problems arise. Consider writing personal letters or making phone calls to at-risk students and their families, explaining that you would like their input on barriers and possible solutions.

Inclusive Schools Action Plan: Practical Steps to Solutions

Schools are in search of progress—progress for students and progress for continuous teacher improvement. Activating progress means getting started planning, writing, and tackling goals. By committing to the concepts in a framework for overcoming cultural mismatch and creating a plan of action, teachers and school leaders can begin the journey toward culturally responsive teaching, thus bringing about real change. Practical steps will lead to positive solutions for marginalized students.

The framework should be considered by district-level and school-level administrators as a self-assessment for overcoming cultural mismatch. Readiness to implement culturally responsive teaching should be established. Administrators should determine the needs of the overall district or individual schools. Goals for schools and teachers can be part of annual or ongoing plans for evaluation, accountability, and improvement. District coordinators and principals should evaluate the current status of culturally responsive practices in their schools and discuss ways for continued success and improvement.

Guided by the inclusive schools action plan in figure 8.2, schools can plan to overcome cultural mismatch and achieve positive outcomes for all students. Creating a plan for inclusion of diversity shows commitment on the part of the school or district to actively become aware of the diverse needs of the student body, address barriers to achievement for marginalized students,

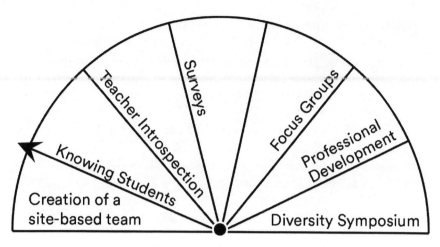

Inclusive Schools Action Plan:
Practical Steps to Solutions

Figure 8.2. **Inclusive Schools Action Plan: Practical Steps to Solutions.**
Source: Laura K. Onuska

and work together to put mechanisms in place that will lead to increased achievement and positive social and emotional development.

The recommendations below are a guide to the process by which school administrators and a site-based team can work to move the needle toward inclusion of diversity in their schools. The team should address the needs of all students in the school, with a specific focus on culturally diverse students, cultural mismatch, and culturally responsive teaching. As the needs of districts and schools vary, teams should decide when and to what extent each recommendation is needed; however, none of the recommendations should be overlooked.

All districts and schools should also consider whether a mechanism is in place for diverse students who move into a less-diverse school. In this way, all districts and schools can utilize an inclusive schools action plan even if their minority population is small. Taking into account the changing demographics of U.S. schools, planning for how to actively include and engage diverse students and overcome cultural mismatch is not a matter of if it will be needed but when.

Create a Site-Based Team for Action Planning

School districts likely already have a team of professionals in place for matters of diversity and protecting civil rights in schools. School-based teams allow the voices of students, teachers, parents, and other school personnel to be heard. The team should plan how to address the needs of the schools and how to implement and measure their plan's effectiveness.

Create a team of individuals who will lead the way and be a driving force at the school. This will include administrators, teachers representative of the grade levels and departments in the school, a school–home liaison if this position exists in the school, students, parents, counselors, and any other individuals deemed pertinent to the particular school. The creation of this team should be shared with a school advisory council or similar group. This is a great time to ask parents of minority students to get involved.

Know Student Demographics

Getting to know your students, their names, and their interests is nothing new. Understanding how they scored on standardized assessments in the previous year is also a common step in identifying what their needs may be in the classroom. In an inclusive schools action plan, the site-based team should create reports that include minority enrollment, percentage of students at each grade level across all demographics, attendance or discipline issues across demographics, and other information important to the particular school like students living in poverty, homelessness, and so on. The team should consider these facts when planning.

Teacher Introspection

The site-based team must make teachers aware of cultural mismatch in the school by sharing reports they create that include student demographics, academic performance, discipline, and attendance. In addition to making school personnel aware of the demographics of the school, the team should define and explain cultural mismatch, encouraging teachers to make self-analysis a part of their preparation for reaching and teaching all students by making time and space for this activity.

Introduce the process of teacher introspection and creating a cultural autobiography. Teams may invite interested faculty members to embark on the process of creating a cultural autobiography or they may plan for the entire staff to participate. Determine what best meets the needs of the school. Several rounds of cultural autobiographies that include all teachers from various grade levels and departments is another path schools may take. Set aside time after participants share their stories for critical discussion. Consider keeping these conversations going through professional learning communities or faculty book study.

Eliciting Voice through Surveys

Eliciting faculty and staff perception of the readiness and utilization of culturally responsive teaching provides the site-based team with additional data. From this data, the team can plan goals, anticipate barriers, design activities, and so on. Appendix G provides sample questions for surveying faculty and staff. Site-based teams should consider adding additional questions that are specific to their site. The team should reassure participants that responses are kept anonymous and confidential.

Even more important than surveying school personnel is the use of surveys for gleaning the perceptions of students, who often are not given a voice in matters of cultural diversity. Sample questions that may be used to elicit student perceptions of their school experience are contained in appendix H. Once the site-based team thoroughly reviews their data for getting to know students, more questions can be added that relate to school-specific issues. Examples include what students may see as solutions for poor attendance or how students think their teachers should react when conflict arises in the classroom.

Focus Groups

The team should consider the benefit of speaking to members of the faculty, student body, and parents. Focus group interviews allow in-depth questioning that goes beyond questionnaires and allow participants to add to others' responses. Results from previously administered surveys can lead team members to generate more-elaborate questions. To form parent-and-family partnerships, the site-based team may choose to host town hall meetings in which the voices of parents and the community are elicited. If a district or school is large, the site-based team members may facilitate multiple focus groups.

Focus group interviews build on survey data received from students and school professionals. For example, a survey question asking students whether teachers get to know the cultures of students may yield yes or no responses; however, in a focus group, the team may choose to ask questions like "What are some barriers that exist to teachers getting to know your culture?" "How important is it to you for your teacher to get to know your cultural background?" or "What are your ideas about how your teacher should learn about your cultural background?"

Another characteristic of focus groups is task orientation. Group members can take on specific problems and work toward solutions. For example, a team may want to conduct a focus group with students and teachers on the issue of attendance. Dedicate time for conversation on the what, why, and how of the issue. Obtain consensus on parameters, or norms, for the meeting like mutual respect, active listening, and keeping time. What better way to solve problems that involve teachers and students than to involve them directly in focused work?

Focus groups can also be used to observe classroom instruction and share reflections. Utilize a protocol specific to the team and what they want to observe. Have a focus group observe teachers committed to equity and culturally responsive teaching. The group can consist of other teachers, students, and an administrator. The purpose of the observation must be determined prior to the observation and in conjunction with the teacher to be observed.

Possible areas to observe include ways the teacher uses students' cultural background in instruction, how the teacher creates a positive classroom environment inclusive of diverse students, how the teachers holds high expectations for all students, and how the teacher resolves conflict. The team can decide whether one or several areas will be included. All participants must know what the areas mean and possible evidence for each.

Walking a focus group through the process of creating a cultural autobiography is another productive activity. Start by asking a number of teachers and students who have a special interest in diversity and social justice to be part of the focus group. The team member leading this task must have directions for creating a cultural autobiography but does not necessarily have to be a school administrator.

Professional Development and Culturally Responsive Teaching
A book-study format is one form of professional development that promotes buy in and may be meaningful for schools. The site-based team reads, studies, and discusses the book. The team could facilitate the same format with the school faculty. To empower teacher leaders and student leaders, an administrator does not have to be the presenter. Each site-based team should consider the cultural background and strength of each of its members to decide what approach to take in the delivery of professional development. If a book study is the decided format, some recommended texts include the following:

- *How to Teach Students Who Don't Look Like You* (Davis, 2012)
- *Facilitators Guide to How to Teach Students Who Don't Look Like You* (Davis, 2008)

- *Courageous Conversations about Race: A Field Guide for Achieving Equity in Schools* (Singleton & Linton, 2014)
- *Facilitator's Guide to Courageous Conversations about Race* (Singleton & Linton, 2006)
- *Culturally Proficient Learning Communities: Confronting Inequities through Collaborative Curiosity* (Lindsey et al., 2009)
- *Culturally Proficient Leadership: The Personal Journey Begins Within* (Terrell, Robins, & Lindsey, 2010)
- *Culturally Responsive Teaching: Theory, Research, and Practice* (Gay, 2010)
- *Culturally Responsive Teaching and the Brain: Promoting Authentic Engagement and Rigor among Culturally and Linguistically Diverse Students* (Hammond, 2015)
- *The Dream-Keepers: Successful Teachers of African American Children* (Ladson-Billings, 2009)
- *We Can't Teach What We Don't Know: White Teachers, Multiracial Schools* (G. Howard, 2006)
- *Strategies and Lessons for Culturally Responsive Teaching: A Primer for K–12 Teachers* (Chartock, 2010)
- *Why Race and Culture Matter in Schools: Closing the Achievement Gap in America's Classrooms* (T. C. Howard, 2010)

Another option for professional development is to have the site-based team present the theory, research, implications, and practices of culturally responsive teaching. This requires that the site-based team choose a title from the list of recommended readings and put a presentation together in a format the team feels would benefit their school. This should include the voices of marginalized students whether in-person or through the use of technology. This promotes buy in among faculty members through showing that there are different sides to every story and that people share beliefs and perceptions that come from their own cultural lens.

Finally, the site-based team might consider inviting or hiring a guest speaker who is an expert in the field, someone to facilitate discussion on diversity and culturally responsive teaching, or prominent community figures of color who have firsthand knowledge and experience of the impact, both positive and negative, of their school experience. Taking into account various ways to format professional development, the site-based team should consider how to best reach their teachers.

Cultural Autobiography Symposium and Discussion

Research shows the meaningfulness and relevance of the cultural autobiography for teachers. Plan for students and parents to engage in the process of writing a cultural autobiography. Encourage interested teachers, school leaders, students, and parents to work through the process and commence critical dialogue and discussion.

The process is a positive way to involve interested stakeholders in confronting cultural mismatch head on. Components of the process include sharing perceptions and beliefs in a safe, constructive setting; listening to one another; identifying similarities and differences; and valuing diverse voices in the school community. Holding a symposium afterward gives those who did not participate in the process an opportunity to see how the process is conducted from beginning to end. Teachers, administrators, students and families from other schools or the community can benefit from attending the symposium.

Several modes for conducting the symposium exist. Participants could share their cultural autobiography in a gallery walk format, displaying their work either on a tri-fold board or via digital technology. As guests circulate, they engage in conversations at their own pace as they view pieces of the cultural autobiography and talk about the process. Another idea is to offer a short presentation in a lecture-format, explaining the process and using visual aids. Finally, the team could host a question-and-answer panel so that guests learn from participants the many facets of the process and have an opportunity to ask questions.

Teacher Preparation Programs

Teacher preparation programs are an ideal setting for aspiring educators to learn about the role an individual's background plays in their view of the world. The earlier preservice teachers learn about the myriad of differences children bring to school with them, the better prepared they will be in reaching and teaching diverse children in public schools and beyond. The goal is for them to avoid experiencing culture shock. They can do this by learning and experiencing students' diverse cultures while working toward meeting beginning teacher benchmarks.

Preservice teachers must take part in a cultural autobiography process in academic coursework. The cultural autobiography alone or a single course on multicultural education or cultural diversity awareness is not sufficient to prepare teachers for effectively teaching the diverse population of students in

U.S. schools; however, it is a start. Every step professors and clinical supervisors can take to embed opportunities for exposure and practice in diverse schools must be taken. Further, discourse and journaling are two ways to include matters related to diversity in program courses and internships.

Suggestions for Additional Research

Further research is needed to understand the level at which schools are effectively practicing culturally responsive teaching. Identifying barriers to the effective utilization of these practices is another focus for further research. School personnel must explore how cultural responsiveness enhances the learning opportunities of students who have historically demonstrated low performance and disengagement.

More work is needed in exploring preservice teachers' perceptions of their preparedness to work with diverse students. Their perception of their role in not fixing underachieving students but placing the "burden of change upon themselves" as teachers (Gay, 2018, p. 289) is another topic to explore. Finally, endeavoring to discover K–12 students' perceptions of their teachers' culturally responsive teaching is another avenue for further study. The following are future research questions to consider:

- How do black and Hispanic students in schools with predominantly white students perceive their teachers' cultural responsiveness in the learning environment?
- How do black and Hispanic students in schools with culturally responsive teachers perform academically compared to black and Hispanic students with a teacher who does not demonstrate culturally responsive practices?
- How do black students in schools with predominantly minority students perceive their teachers' cultural responsiveness in the learning environment?
- How do black and Hispanic students in schools with predominantly black and Hispanic students perceive their teachers' cultural responsiveness in the learning environment?
- How do black and Hispanic students in a classroom with a culturally responsive teacher perform on standardized assessments compared to black and Hispanic students not in the teacher's classroom?

Teachers' readiness to begin culturally responsive teaching should be further explored. Teachers are the first contact and interaction with students, thus making the first impression. How teachers understand or approach the need for and implementation of culturally responsive teaching needs further attention.

Members of the site based teams may want to create additional avenues for action research that would benefit their specific school. For example, the team could study the effect of affirming teacher behavior in high school as a way to strengthen teacher–student relationships and improve attendance. Another example is determining how high expectations are communicated to all students in elementary school. Allocating time and resources to action research in diversity and social justice, the administrator of the school demonstrates commitment to ongoing problem solving to help marginalized students overcome barriers.

Conclusion

The suggestions in this chapter offer practical approaches with workable action steps. The goal is to energize your staff to begin to listen to and seek to understand the voices of marginalized groups of students. Diverging from division, blame, and excuses, school professionals must look inward to develop empathy outwardly. Using these implementation recommendations, teachers and school leaders can readily begin to take action.

In a framework for overcoming cultural mismatch, teachers have a tool for stepping out of their comfort zone and committing to a shift in thinking. Knowing students, participating in introspection, and partnering with parents are action steps all teachers ought to make a priority. Administrators must support teachers by understanding and applying the tenets of culturally responsive teaching, recruiting and retaining minority teachers, and initiating or further enhancing innovative partnerships with families and community organizations who value the same mission.

An inclusive schools action plan allows schools to begin to move the needle toward recognizing and applying the tenets of culturally responsive teaching. Through first building a site-based team representative of student body demographics and comprised of students, teachers, and other stakeholders, the school prepares to usher in a change in thinking about diversity and the needs of marginalized students and the responsibility of teachers and school leaders.

Key elements of the plan include knowing students, encouraging teacher introspection, conducting surveys of faculty and students, holding focus groups, providing training on culturally responsive teaching, and hosting a symposium. Teams decide how and when to take action, communicating goals as well as progress to stakeholders as they help to develop a sense of urgency among school professionals to effect change. Improved academic performance and increased social well-being as evidenced by improved discipline and attendance will result.

Teacher preparation programs are the most integral component of preparing culturally responsive teachers. University and college faculty should provide the knowledge and skills needed and opportunities for practice. Diverse teaching settings are crucial if the preservice teacher is to become a well-informed teacher ready to reach and teach all students regardless of cultural differences. Encouraging students to take on diverse teaching experiences while also completing a cultural autobiography enables all teachers to develop empathy and understanding of students' cultural lenses and their respective voices.

Scholars and school professionals alike should pursue further research. Action research is a crucial component of exploring issues facing student achievement in schools. Arriving at solutions is very meaningful when the researchers are the teachers and administrators themselves. Students, parents, and others on the site-based team should also be included in the research process.

CHAPTER NINE

~

Conclusion

Cultural mismatch refers to the difference between a student's cultural background and that of his or her assigned teacher. Overcoming cultural mismatch is a feat that school leaders should take on now. Students in U.S. public schools come from all walks of life. They practice different religions, belong to different ethnic groups, have different ancestral histories, have certain customs and value systems, and so on. They experience the world around them through their own cultural lens. Including their cultural background with care and diligence will lead to positive outcomes in both academic achievement and social and emotional development.

Changing demographics call all stakeholders to action. Improving opportunities for underrepresented populations is attainable. School leaders who are willing to utilize a framework for overcoming cultural mismatch and create an inclusive action plan will begin to improve school experiences for marginalized students. Advocates for culturally responsive teaching have been bringing cultural mismatch to light for years. Its inequities can no longer be ignored.

The achievement gap of minority and white students remains a pressing issue for schools. While black and Hispanic students have made some improvement along with white students on the NAEP in recent years, gap scores between these student subgroups still remain significant. Narrowing the achievement gap requires that dedicated educators acknowledge the role cultural frames of reference play in learning and development. Academic achievement and social and emotional growth cannot be fostered without cultural connections.

Reducing the negative effect of cultural mismatch on marginalized students is attainable. Gathering the collective voices of students, teachers, and principals, Fuller (2014) sought to determine perceptions of culturally responsive teaching in low-performing schools in the southeastern United States. The themes reported across cases showed promising evidence of culturally responsive practices in four separate cases in one school district.

All of the teachers and students identified evidence of developing high expectations for all students, promoting parental involvement, and acknowledging and welcoming students' diverse cultural backgrounds. The main themes emerged from student responses across all cases, and these were confirmed by teachers' responses. Student perceptions of their abilities and preparedness to meet high expectations all related to the teacher's role in explicitly stating these high expectations, supporting their needs, caring for them, and providing rigorous classwork.

Students in these cases perceived that teachers hold them to high expectations, provide rigorous classwork, and are supportive. Students also perceived that culturally responsive teachers valued parent involvement, took the time to reach out to parents, and students felt that they could improve in school with parental support and involvement. All students perceived teachers as acknowledging cultural differences. Yet, inquiring about students' cultural backgrounds and incorporating some aspects of culture in the classroom were not shared perceptions of students.

A teacher who is culturally responsive begins by acknowledging the importance of the student and the family's culture. Communicating with parents to help the student have a positive school experience is another attribute. Students across cases agreed that they want to see their teacher and parents communicating. Student-led conferences were seen by both the students and the teachers as an opportunity to show pride in their work, and everyone agreed that parents should also know about discipline problems and academic underachievement as well.

Students perceived that cultural backgrounds were incorporated in the classroom but was mostly limited to occasional discussions or comments about diverse cultures when presented in the curriculum. Students thought teachers were interested in their cultures, although not all were sure their teachers actually knew about them. Teachers offered limited responses on how they incorporated student culture; however, they all valued the students' diverse backgrounds, demonstrated care and concern for them individually, and acknowledged that students' cultural backgrounds contributed to learning styles and how they approach learning (Fuller 2014).

Adding to the body of research on preservice teachers' voices, a separate study was conducted (see chapter 7). This case study was conducted with preservice teachers at a private, religious university in the southeastern United States to explore the beliefs and perceptions of preservice teachers on writing their first cultural autobiography. Additionally, preservice teachers were asked to reflect on their preparedness to teach culturally diverse students and students living in poverty. Eight students participated in an initial questionnaire and three white, female, senior education majors participated in further questioning.

The themes that emerged included meaning, need, and relevance. Participants valued the experience of introspection. They noted a positive experience sharing and discussing their cultural autobiographies with peers. They agreed the process is needed as they prepare to become teachers, sharing that it added to their readiness to work with students of all backgrounds. Continued introspection and discourse coupled with opportunities to teach in diverse settings must be incorporated in all teacher preparation programs, and this is encouraged for new teacher programs in school districts, faculty development, and interested special interest groups.

Both studies add to the research on equity in education. They showcase that schools need to have mechanisms in place for overcoming cultural mismatch. These include a framework outlining teacher and administrator roles, action planning for including diversity, considerations for teacher preparation programs, and continued research. Intentionally planning for inclusiveness in schools through conscious action on the part of administrators and teachers leads to positive outcomes for minority students, who for far too long have been marginalized.

Implementing a framework for overcoming cultural mismatch will allow schools to take action. Learning about students, writing a cultural autobiography, and partnering with parents are all crucial points of focus for teachers. As school leaders work with teachers on this, they should also promote culturally responsive teaching practices and focus on increasing minority teacher recruitment and retention and building family and community partnerships.

Through the use of an inclusive schools action plan, members of a site-based team can work to move the needle toward school environments that actively implement practices inclusive of diversity. Team members share this responsibility as collective voices working for social justice. Tasks of the plan include student and staff surveys, teacher introspection, focus groups, professional development on culturally responsive teaching, and symposiums that celebrate diversity. Teachers, school leaders, and the faculty of teacher preparation programs must realize a sense of urgency and respond.

Advocating for marginalized students is more important than ever. Each professional at every school can do his or her part in solving this ongoing issue in education. Teachers and school leaders should participate in self-analysis by creating a cultural autobiography. While the journey to cultural competence and culturally responsive teaching requires a shift in thinking, it is attainable. To become the most effective teacher of diverse students, start with a look at your own self. This is just one step in the right direction. It is a crucial and vital step, a step in the right direction toward reaching and teaching all children.

∼

Create Your Cultural Autobiography

Open the Door to
Culturally Responsive Teaching

Directions: Consider the following questions. Record your reflections in the written or digital format of your choice. Include personal pictures if you wish. Share and discuss.

Basic Questions (Surface)

Describe the type of school you attended.
Was your schooling experience positive, neutral, or negative? Why?
How did your family identify ethnically or racially?*
Where did you live—an urban, suburban, or rural community?*
Were you born in the United States?
What is the story of your family in America? Has your family been here for generations, a few decades, or a few years?*
What are your customs and beliefs?
What are some of your family traditions—holidays, foods, or rituals?*
Who were the heroes celebrated in your family or community? Why? Who were the antiheroes? Who were the bad guys?*
How was education valued as you were growing up?
What is the education level of your parents? Grandparents?
Were you the first in your family to attend college? If not, who did—your parents, grandparents, or great-grandparents?*
Do you speak another language? Is it your native language?
Were other languages spoken in your home when you were growing up?

What family folklore or stories did you regularly hear growing up?*
How would you describe your family's socioeconomic status—middle class, upper class, working class, or low income? What does that mean in terms of quality of life?*

Additional Questions (Going Deeper)

What family stories are regularly told or referenced? What message do they communicate about core values?*

Review primary messages from your upbringing. What did your parents, neighbors, and other authority figures tell you respect looked like? Disrespect?*

How were you trained to respond to different emotional displays—crying, anger, and happiness?*

What physical, social, or cultural attributes were praised in your community? Which ones were you taught to avoid?*

How were you expected to interact with authority figures? Was the authority of teachers and other elders assumed or did it have to be earned?*

As a child, did you call adults by their first name? Why?

What earned you praise as a child?*

How do you get to know the cultures of the students in your classroom?

How do you incorporate your students' cultures in teaching and learning?

Do your students know their cultures are important?

How does your culture inform your instructional decision making?

How does your culture inform your classroom management and disciplinary procedures?

*Denotes question taken directly from Hammond (2015, p. 57).

APPENDIX B

Sample Artifact

My Family's Cultural Background

My Family's Cultural Background

White American

Dad's side is mostly German + partly Jewish from my grandma

Mom's side is English, Welsh, Dutch, and Irish

My family has lived in America for around 4-5 generations. My great great great great (and possibly more) grandparents on my dad's side came to America from Germany

APPENDIX C

Sample Artifact

Culture

CULTURE

- Though my mom is from Canada and my dad's parents are from the Philippines, I was raised without much cultural variation from what is considered typically American.
  - I learned that the term "white-washed" describes this
  - I never had Filipino food until high school
- Never been to the Philippines, but I've been to Montreal a lot
- My mom, and sometimes my dad, always cooked, so I didn't really learn how at home

APPENDIX D

~

Sample Artifact

School Experience

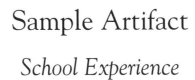

SCHOOL EXPERIENCE IMPACTED BY:

race/ethnicity	Social Class	Religion

race/ethnicity

Positive
+Though strict, my mother taught us to always be kind. You can be kind to all, but you do not have to befriend all.
+Being hispanic did not really impact my schooling, but it did help growing up bilingual to help communicate with or for others.

Negative
-Very Strict household in terms of social limitations
-Growing up speaking spanglish hindered my reading and writing abilities. While I still passed with A's, I struggled with correct spelling, reading, and even mixing in spanish terms with english ones when communicating.
-

Social Class

Positive
+My social Class influenced me to be more aware, empathetic, and caring to all...
+Influenced my thought to a most grateful and positive one

Negative
-We moved a lot during school, renting house to house.
-Stability in the home was mediocre.
-Mother and Father are Separated made influenced me emotionally and other situations led to insecurity.

Religion

Positive
+my moral groundings that I grew to form from Catholic doctrine really helped me make my own decisions and stand my ground under the influence of others.
+Has helped me to be kind and influenced positively the way I see and interact with others

Negative
-it is difficult having a view different than others and sometimes succumbing to being reserved and quiet about my beliefs occured.

APPENDIX E

~

Sample Artifact

My Ethnic Background

MY ETHNIC BACKGROUND

- European American
- Cuban American
- Texan

APPENDIX F

Sample Artifact

Diversity

DIVERSITY

- I was not exposed to much diversity of race, ethnicity, class, or beliefs throughout my childhood
- The importance of diversity and culture has never specifically been a topic of discussion in my family, however, my parents have always stressed the fact that every human being is made in the image and likeness of God, and therefore has the dignity that is inherent from that

APPENDIX G

~

Sample Faculty Survey

1. What is your teaching background (university internships, diverse teaching experiences, subjects, and grades)?
2. What are the key attributes that your students need in you as a teacher?
3. Using only five words, how would your students describe you?
4. In your opinion, what makes a teacher great?
5. What makes a school great?
6. When do you know your students are successful?
7. How do they feel and act when they have achieved? How do you celebrate their successes?
8. What expectations do you have for your students?
9. How do you meet the diverse learning needs of your students?
10. Can you explain some engaging lessons or activities?
11. How do you come to know what they need?
12. How do you plan for what culturally diverse students need?
13. How do you know they have learned?
14. In what ways do you incorporate the cultural backgrounds and experiences of your students?
15. In terms of classroom management, are there ways you are culturally sensitive?
16. When choosing curriculum and planning lessons, how is cultural diversity accounted for?
17. What value do you see in parent involvement?

18. Describe how teachers should interact with and include parents and families.
19. How do you include parents and families and their cultural backgrounds?
20. Can you please give me the approximate demographic composition of the students in your class?
21. About how many students in your class would you say receive free or reduced lunch?
22. What effects of poverty are evident in the lives of your students?
23. How does that affect their learning and school experience?
24. How do you handle that and accommodate those needs?
25. Is there anything else you would like to share about responding to students' cultural background in the teaching and learning process?

Sample Student Survey

1. What does your teacher expect you to learn and be able to do?
2. How do you know?
3. What do you expect to learn or be able to do?
4. How do you feel about school?
5. Do you like school? Why or why not?
6. Are you shown respect? What does respect mean to you?
7. In your opinion, what makes a teacher great?
8. What does he or she say and do?
9. How does he or she act when teaching, when interacting with students, when interacting with parents?
10. When do you feel successful at school?
11. How do you act or feel when you have achieved?
12. How does your teacher celebrate your successes or other students' successes?
13. Does your teacher hold high expectations for all the students in your class? How do you know?
14. What are some examples?
15. Does he or she have the same goals for all students?
16. Does he or she think all students can do their best?
17. Describe your culture.
18. What does the teacher do to include your culture in the classroom and in your learning experience?
19. How would you like your culture to be included in your classroom?

20. Does your teacher know about your culture?
21. Would you like him or her to know about your culture?
22. What would you like him or her to know?
23. Has your teacher ever spoken with your parents?
24. Have your parents attended school conferences?
25. How do you feel about your teacher and your parent speaking?
26. Do you think it is important for your teacher and your parents to speak?
27. Do you do better, worse, or the same in school when your parents and your teacher speak?
28. Is there anything else you would like to include?

Bibliography

Barton, P. E., & Coley, R. J. (2010). The black–white achievement gap: When progress stopped. *Educational Testing Service Policy Evaluation and Research Center*, 1–40.

Bohrnstedt, G., Kitmitto, S., Ogut, B., Sherman, D., & Chan, D. (2015). *School composition and the black–white achievement gap* (NCES 2015-018). Washington, DC: National Center for Education Statistics. http://nces.ed.gov/pubsearch.

Brown-Jeffy, S., & Cooper, J. E. (2011). Toward a conceptual framework of culturally relevant pedagogy: An overview of the conceptual and theoretical literature. *Teacher Education Quarterly*, 38(1), 65–84.

Carver-Thomas, D. (2018). *Diversifying the teaching profession: How to recruit and retain teachers of color.* Palo Alto, CA: Learning Policy Institute.

Chartock, R. K. (2010). *Strategies and lessons for culturally responsive teaching: A primer for K–12 teachers.* Boston, MA: Pearson.

Chavez, A. F., & Guido-DiBrito, F. (1999). Racial and ethnic identity and development. *New Directions for Adult and Continuing Education*, 84, 39–47.

Cho, G., & DeCastro-Ambrosetti, D. (2005). Is ignorance bliss? Preservice teachers' attitudes toward multicultural education. *High School Journal*, 89(2), 24–28.

Dana, N. F., & Yendol-Hoppey, D. (2020). *The reflective educator's guide to classroom research: Learning to teach and teaching to learn through practitioner inquiry* (4th edition). Thousand Oaks, CA: Corwin Press.

Davis, B. M. (2012). *How to teach students who don't look like you: Culturally responsive teaching strategies* (2nd edition). Thousand Oaks, CA: Corwin Press.

Decuir-Gunby, J. T., DeVance Taliaferro, J., & Greenfield, D. (2010). Educator's perspectives on culturally relevant programs for academic success: The American Excellence Association. *Education and Urban Society*, 42(2), 182–204.

Edwards, C. E. (2010). Cultural responsiveness in three programs for African American students. (Doctoral dissertation). ProQuest, 3404537.

Egalite, A. J., and Kisida, B. (2018). The effects of teacher match on students' academic perceptions and attitudes. *Educational Evaluation and Policy Analysis*, 40(1): 59–81.

Egalite, A. J., Kisida, B., & Winters, M. A. (2015). Representation in the classroom: The effect of own-race teachers on student achievement. *Economics of Education Review*, 45, 44–52.

Florida Department of Education. (2020). Staff in Florida's Public Schools, District Reports 2019–2020: Instructional Staff. www.fldoe.org/accountability/data-sys/edu-info-accountability-services/pk-12-public-school-data-pubs-reports/archive.stml.

Fuller, A. L. (2014). Listening to the student voice: An exploration of students' perceptions of their teachers' cultural responsiveness. (Doctoral dissertation). ProQuest, 3716855.

Gay, G. (2000). *Culturally responsive teaching: Theory, research, and practice* (2nd edition). New York: Teachers College.

———. (2002). Preparing for culturally responsive teaching. *Journal of Teacher Education*, 53(2), 106–16.

———. (2018). *Culturally responsive teaching: Theory, research, and practice* (3rd edition). New York: Teachers College.

Gunn, A. A., Bennett, S. V., Shuford Evans, L., Peterson, B. J., & Welsh, J. L. (2013). Autobiographies in preservice teacher education: A snapshot tool for building a culturally relevant pedagogy. *International Journal of Multicultural Education*, 15(1), 1–20.

Hammond, Z. L. (2015). *Culturally responsive teaching and the brain: Promoting authentic engagement and rigor among culturally and linguistically diverse students.* Thousand Oaks, CA: Corwin Press.

Hemphill, F. C., & Vanneman, A. (2011). *Achievement gaps: How Hispanic and white students in public schools perform in mathematics and reading on the National Assessment of Educational Progress* (NCES 2011-459). Washington, DC: National Center for Education Statistics.

Howard, G. (2006). *We can't teach what we don't know: White teachers, multiracial schools* (2nd edition). New York: Teachers College.

Howard, T. C. (2001). Telling their side of the story: African American students' perceptions of culturally relevant teaching. *Urban Review*, 33(2), 131–49.

———. (2003). Culturally relevant pedagogy: Ingredients for critical teacher reflection. *Theory into Practice*, 42(3), 195–202.

———. (2010). *Why race and culture matter in schools: Closing the achievement gap in America's Classrooms.* New York: Teachers College.

Hughes, C., Page, A., & Ford, D. Y. (2011). Cultural dynamics in an economically challenged, multi-ethnic middle school: Student perceptions. *Journal of At-Risk Issues*, 16(1), 9–16.

Kalman, B. (2009). *What is culture?* New York: Crabtree Publishing.

Kim, Y. & Baylor, A. (2006). A social-cognitive framework for pedagogical agents as learning companions. *Educational Technology Research and Development, 52,* 569–96.

Ladson-Billings, G. (1995). Toward a theory of culturally relevant pedagogy. *American Education Research Journal, 32*(3), 465–91.

———. (2007). Pushing past the achievement gap. *Journal of Negro Education, 76*(3), 316–23.

———. (2009). *The dreamkeepers: Successful teaching for African American students.* San Francisco: Jossey-Bass.

Lindsey, D. B., Jungwirth, L. D., Pahl, J. V. N. C., & Lindsey, R. B. (2009). *Culturally proficient learning communities: Confronting inequities through collaborative curiosity.* Thousand Oaks, CA: Corwin Press.

Moore, A. L. (2007). Guess who's coming to dinner: The importance of multiculturalism in the aftermath of Hurricane Katrina. *Multicultural Education, 15*(2), 24–30.

Morrison, K. A., Robbins, H. H., & Rose, D. G. (2008). Operationalizing culturally relevant pedagogy: A synthesis of classroom-based research. *Equity and Excellence in Education, 41*(4), 433–52.

Narváez, D., Constanza, N., Lastra Ramírez, S. P., & Morales Vasco, A. M. (2013). Autobiographies: A way to explore student teachers' beliefs in a teacher education program. *Profile Issues in Teachers' Professional Development, 15*(2), 35–47. www.scielo.org.co/scielo.php?script=sci_arttext&pid=S1657-07902013000200003&lng=en&tlng=en.

National Assessment of Educational Progress. (2019). The nation's report card. www.nationsreportcard.gov.

National Center for Education Statistics. (2011). The condition of education 2011. https://nces.ed.gov/pubs2011/2011033_1.pdf.

———. (2012). The condition of education 2012. https://nces.ed.gov/pubs2012/2012045.pdf.

———. (2019). Projections of education statistics to 2027. https://nces.ed.gov/pubs2019/2019001.pdf

Pajares, F. (2002). Overview of social cognitive theory and of self-efficacy. www.uky.edu/~eushe2/Pajares/eff.html.

Parhar, N., & Sensoy, O. (2011). Culturally relevant pedagogy redux: Canadian teachers' conceptions of their work and its challenges. *Canadian Journal of Education, 34*(2), 189–218.

Popp, P. A., Grant, L. W., & Stronge, J. H. (2011). Effective teachers for at-risk or highly mobile students: What are the dispositions and behaviors of award-winning teachers? *Journal of Education for Students Placed at Risk, 16*(4), 275–91.

Shealey, M. W., & Callins, T. (2007). Creating culturally responsive literacy programs in inclusive classrooms. *Intervention in School and Clinic, 42*(4), 195–97.

Singleton, G. E., & Linton, C. (2014). *Courageous conversations about race: A field guide for achieving equity in schools* (2nd edition). Thousand Oaks, CA: Corwin Press.

Siwatu, K. O. (2007). Preservice teachers' culturally responsive teaching self-efficacy and outcome expectancy beliefs. *Teaching and Teacher Education*, 23, 1,086–1,101.

Sleeter, C. E. (2011). An agenda to strengthen culturally responsive pedagogy. *English Teaching: Practice & Critique*, 10(2), 7–23.

Soumah, M. A., & Hoover, J. H. (2013). A conversation on equality with students of color. *Reclaiming Children and Youth*, 22(1), 18–23.

Terrell, R. D., Robins, K. N., & Lindsey, R. B. (2009). *Culturally proficient leadership: The personal journey begins within*. Thousand Oaks, CA: Corwin Press.

Toney, M. R. (2009). Pedagogical beliefs and practices of culturally responsive teachers of African American students. (Doctoral dissertation). ProQuest, 3391086.

U.S. Department of Education. (2014). 2013–14 state and national estimations. https://ocrdata.ed.gov/estimations/2013-2014.

Villegas, A. M., & Lucas, T. (2002). Preparing culturally responsive teachers: Rethinking the curriculum. *Journal of Teacher Education*, 53(1), 30–32.

Walker, K. L. (2011). Deficit thinking and the effective teacher. *Education and Urban Society*, 43(5), 576–97.

Wong, P. (2008). Transactions, transformation, and transcendence: Multicultural service-learning experience of preservice teachers. *Multicultural Education*, 16(2), 31–36.

~

About the Author

Abigail L. Fuller is assistant professor of elementary education and chairperson of the Education Department at Ave Maria University (AMU) in South Florida. She was a Champions for Learning Teacher of Distinction in 2009. Fuller has presented at the 2019 Kappa Delta Pi Convocation in Norfolk, Virginia; the 2020 Southwest Florida TESOL Conference in Fort Myers, Florida; and the 2020 Florida Sunshine State TESOL Virtual Conference. She earned a bachelor of science degree in elementary education and dance, with a minor in special education, from Slippery Rock University in Pennsylvania; a master of education degree in school leadership from Florida Gulf Coast University; and a doctorate in school administration from the University of Florida.

Fuller's preservice teaching experiences included the Urban Student Teaching Program in conjunction with Pittsburgh Public Schools; the Urban Teaching Seminar in Philadelphia; and missions work teaching English and dance in Zacapa, Guatemala. In addition to her role as a clinical supervisor at AMU, she teaches courses on educational foundations; classroom management and organization; teaching diverse and exceptional students; measurement and assessment in the classroom; teaching math in the elementary classroom; and teaching science in the elementary classroom.